W0391225

AURICULAS

AURICULAS

Their Care and Cultivation

BRENDA HYATT

CASSELL · LONDON

First published in 1989 by
Cassell, Artillery House
Artillery Row, London SW1 1RT

British Library Cataloguing in Publication Data
Hyatt, Brenda
Auriculas
1. Auriculas Cultivation
I. Title
635.9′33672

ISBN 0 304 32245 8

Produced by Justin Knowles Publishing Group
9 Colleton Crescent, Exeter EX2 4BY

Editor: Roy Gasson
Design: Michael Head
Line illustrations: David Ashby

Typeset by Keyspools Ltd
Printed and bound in Hong Kong

CONTENTS

LIST OF PLATES

Foreword

Its range of colour must place the florist's auricula in a class of its own; there can be no other plant with such varied and charming shades. It is this, I am sure, that has made auriculas great favourites wherever they are seen.

The true lover of auriculas sees beauty in them all the year round, not just when they are flowering. The colour and form of the leaves are as diverse as those of the flowers and they give pleasure throughout all seasons. The crisp green leaves of the alpines and the silver-grey or intense frosty white leaves of the shows make for a great variety of shades during the flowerless seasons. The leaf edges – some entire and others deeply toothed – also add variety as well as charm. With this disposition to vary, auriculas never cease to be a joy.

My grandfather's auricula collection was considered to be, from the late 19th century on, by far the finest in Great Britain – a standard that was maintained by my father and by me until my recent retirement. I am delighted that the collection is now in the care of Brenda Hyatt; she is a well-known exhibitor and I know of no more dedicated grower. It is her total dedication to auriculas that has solved the many difficulties confronting her in continually housing her collection of plants. She has put to full use the space available to her with an ingenuity that could only have been achieved by someone determined to find a way to succeed in a worthwhile task. Her resolution has ensured her continued success as a leading grower and exhibitor.

Her knowledge and expertise uniquely qualify her to write this comprehensive book about the auricula: I am delighted to welcome it.

GORDON DOUGLAS

Introduction

During many years of growing and exhibiting auriculas, I have received a continuous avalanche of letters from amateur growers asking for cultural information, because many would-be enthusiasts feel that auriculas may be difficult plants to grow. I fully understand this apprehension and it is with the inexperienced grower very much in mind that I have written this book.

I came upon the auricula purely by chance. I had joined a family-owned alpine-plant nursery and worked there with a wide range of plants. The tasks involved – moving plants from frame to bench to show and back again for repotting – were absorbing in their way and I had my favourites among the plants. Then, one day, a box of show auriculas in full bloom arrived at the nursery and all thoughts of the job in hand vanished. I was completely mesmerized by the beauty of those auriculas. My first feelings were of disbelief in their reality. The delicate, porcelain-like flowers, with their velvety greens, greys, reds, and purples, along with so many other rich colours, seemed like paintings come to life.

Those first auriculas cast a lasting spell over me; from that day on my interest in them became single-minded, almost obsessive.

Like other enthusiasts before and since, I was afraid that their cultivation would be difficult, or beyond my experience at that time, but I soon found that their cultural demands were few and uncomplicated – their greatest needs were fresh air and commonsense treatment. The clue lies in their mountain origins, which should always be remembered if the temptation to cosset the plants arises.

There are many reasons for growing and raising auriculas. It may be the simple pleasure of having this beautiful plant in your garden that spurs you on, or the wish to raise something new, or the desire to win a premier award on the showbench. Whatever the reason, you may be sure that taking on the challenge of this jewel among flowers will bring nothing but surprise and pleasure along the way.

The whole delight and accommodating nature of the auricula was summed up by a British writer, John Laurance, over two hundred and fifty years ago, in 1726:

> The Auricula or Bear's Ear is justly valued and esteemed by all Florists. For Nature nowhere discovers her Variety of Colours, her Shades and pretty Mixtures more than in this little Flower, which is raised both from the Seed, and from Slips. In the former Way have been raised of late years a surprizing Variety of Sorts, which the Editor by Way of Boasting and triumph Names after some great Family or conspicuous Person. In the latter Way you are sure to preserve and propagate the Sort, with a little care in removing and parting the Roots whilst they are in Flower.
>
> Those who are curious in the preserving and boldly explaining the best Sorts put them in Pots, the better to preserve them both in Summer and Winter. For the Auricula is a plant that delights in the Shade; and too much Wet is apt to rot it in the Winter, and in the Summer to take off that beautiful Powder which so much adorns the Flower, and graces the Eye of it. . . .

I

ORIGINS AND HISTORY

The auriculas we know today, with their unforgettable perfume and beauty, bear little resemblance to their forebears of centuries ago. The hybrids now exhibited are the results of many years' dedicated artistry by florists through the ages, always striving for perfection.

The auricula is a true antique among cultivated flowers. Its origins go back to the mountainous regions of Europe, and the ancestors of today's auriculas seem to be one hybrid and two species. The natural hybrid, *Primula × pubescens*, grows quite happily in the European Alps, its flowers varying from purple shades through to white. It is probably a hybrid between *P. rubra* and *P. auricula*, both of which have features inherent in *P. × pubescens*. *P. rubra* usually has flowers of a bright rose colour, although the occasional white or lavender flower is seen. *P. auricula* has yellow flowers and in addition a light ring of farina forms an attractive white eye in the centre of each flower. These characteristics are present in the border and show auriculas we know today, while the alpine auricula (now a classified hybrid form) completely lacks farina and has characteristics similar to those in *P. × pubescens*.

The true history of the auricula, though, is the history of the florists who created it. For the auricula we know today is a man-made plant. It is the work of generations of florists, using that word in its true sense of persons who cultivated decorative flowering plants, grew them to a high standard of excellence, and, as time went on, tested them by exhibiting them in competition with fellow florists.

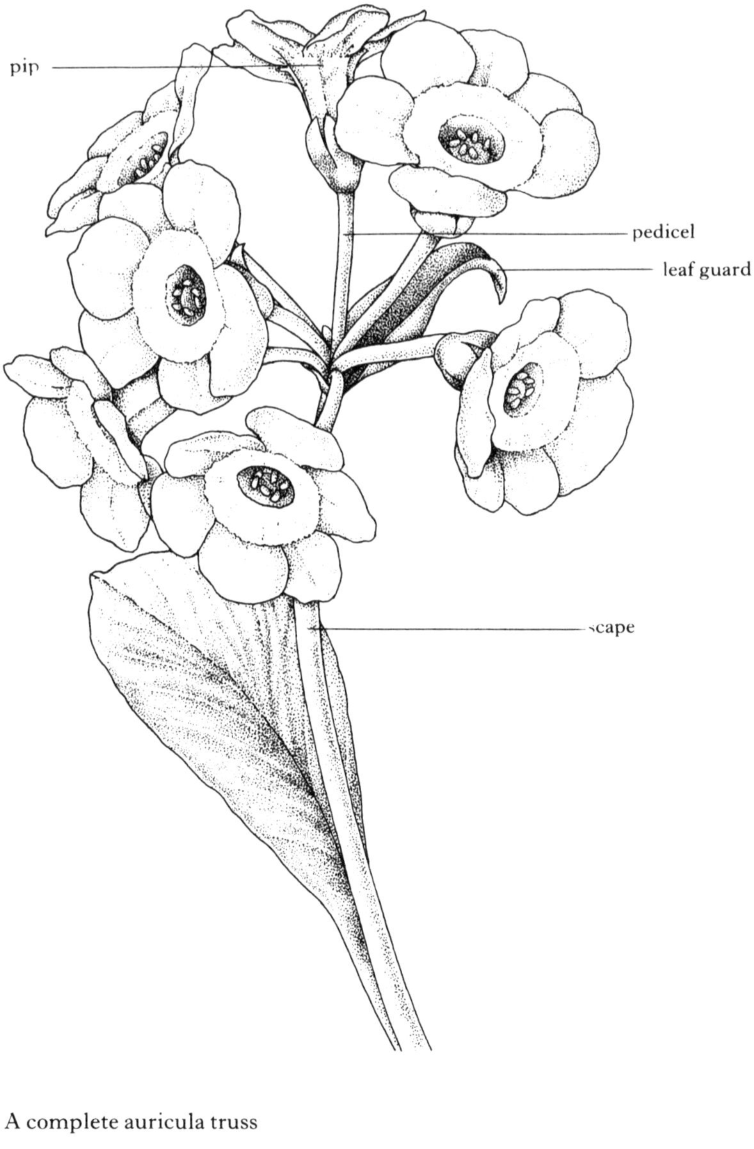

A complete auricula truss

The first mentions of auriculas in the English-speaking world date from the 16th century. In his *Herball*, published in 1596, the English botanist John Gerard referred to auriculas; he called them 'beare's eares' or 'mountain cowslips'. But the flower must have been known before Gerard's time by florists in continental Europe. Gaspard Bauhin, in his *Phytophinax* of 1569, notes 12 varieties. He called the plant 'auricula ursi', which translates as 'the bear's little ear'. The reference is, presumably, to the leaf shape.

Gerard and other writers of this period placed great emphasis on the medicinal value of plants. I cannot resist quoting three passages about the auricula:

> The Swiss called them 'Schwindlekraut' and used the rootes for strengthening of the head, so when they are on top of places that are high 'giddiness' and the swimming of the 'braine' may not affect them.
>
> They does all call it Paralytica because of his virtues in curing the palsies, cramps and convulsions. The rootes ... taking in the way of one or two drams, helpeth such as have devoured the Sea Hare, or have been bitten by a Toad, or taken too great a quantity of opium ....
>
> The Swiss eat rootes of Auriculas before climbing mountains to prevent loss of use of 'neckes'.

Even in these early times growers were improving the stock. In Gerard's *Herball* there are drawings showing small flowerheads with only four pips. Yet a little more than 30 years later, John Parkinson, 'Herbalist' to King Charles I, in his *Paradisi in Sole Paradisus,* published in 1629, describes the successful raising of new varieties. He says that they are too numerous to describe, but a drawing in his book – of 'the greatest faire bear's ears with eyes' – illustrates a vast step forward. The flowers are easily three times the size of those in Gerard's book and there were as many as thirteen flowering pips to a stem. Parkinson also described two distinct types of foliage, one with powdery meal, the other completely clear.

Clusius, botanist to the Emperor Maximillian II, had already described six species in 1583. He first saw auriculas in the garden of an old friend, Professor C. V. Aichholz of Vienna, who had been given plants that had been found growing in the Alps near Innsbruck. Aichholz sent some plants to Clusius, who grew successfully, in the emperor's gardens in Vienna, 'Auricula ursi I', the yellow *P. auricula*, and 'Auricula ursi II', the hybrid *P.* × *pubescens.* His success led to these plants being distributed far and wide throughout Europe.

Auriculas had certainly reached England by 1633, the year in which Thomas Johnson edited a new edition of Gerard's *Herball.* Johnson mentions many auriculas grown by John Tradescant, gardener to Charles I, among his collection of rare plants in his garden at Lambeth and acknowledges the improvements Tradescant had bred into them. He also noted that auriculas were to be found in the garden of a Mr Tuggie. 'Of the floures', he wrote, 'some are fairer than othersome, and their colours are so various that it is hard to find words to express them'.

John Parkinson, in his *Theatrum Botanicum* (1640), describes some auriculas as 'variously stript with a kind of whitish bluish colour ... ', so we now see striping making its debut upon the auricula scene.

Sir Thomas Hanmer, in his *Garden Book* completed in 1659 but published only in 1933, described the ever-widening colour range available by the middle of the 17th century: 'We have whites, yellows of all sorts, haire colours, oranges, cherry colours, crimson and other reds, violets, purples, murreys, tawneys, olives, cinnamon colours, ash colour, dunns, and whatnot ... '. Thomas Hanmer was a skilled gardener and, with seed sowing now common practice, he was obviously extremely successful in the raising of new varieties. One quite dramatic plant was named 'Black Imperial' – apparently the darker the flower, the more highly desirable it became. Another, raised in 'Battersey near London', had the charming name of 'Mistris Buggs her Fine Purple'.

Double auriculas had put in their appearance by 1665. It is difficult to translate their value into today's terms, but one nurseryman sold auriculas in pots for one shilling and doubles for four shillings. It is reported that a short time later a striped auricula was sold for £20.

If this is true then auriculas were now among the elite of plants. There was an increasing awareness by nurserymen of the high value placed on novelties they had either bred, perhaps accidentally, or bought from amateur growers.

The university city of Oxford has the oldest botanic garden in England. This garden, established in 1621, was founded by Lord Danby and from 1632 was in the skilled hands of Jacob Bobart. A book containing the lists Bobart made of 1,600 plants in his care is still preserved in the botanic library at Oxford. The *Catalogus Plantarum Horti Medici Oxoniensis*, dated 1648, contains descriptions alongside each plant name. Nine auriculas are named and described. A striped purple 'beare's eare' appeared. It seems that by now striped and purple shades were preferred to yellows.

Continuous selection had resulted in improvements, and a standard of excellence was emerging on to the scene. This was evidenced in John Rea's *Flora, or a Complete Florilege*, published in 1702, which encouraged many more amateurs to test their skills. Rules enabled comparisons to be made between flowers shown by rival collectors and florists of the day were then able to select plants nearest in quality to those desired standards.

A few years ago, by request, I planted some of my auriculas in a private garden of the French Hospital in Rochester in southeast England. This was in preparation for the celebration in 1985 held to commemorate the tercentenary of the revocation of the Edict of Nantes. My plants duly took their place alongside many other kinds, each chosen because it had had its place in French history over 300 years ago.

I felt then that I had been caught up in the tradition recorded in many old books that auriculas had been brought to England by Flemish weavers or other refugees. When these refugees fled to England's industrial north, their work involved long hours at their looms and they sought relaxation in their gardens, looking after auriculas they had brought with them.

In the 17th and 18th centuries auriculas became popular subjects for Flemish painters. Earlier paintings show little richness of colour in these auriculas, but a painting of a striped variety by Paul-Theodor van Brussel (1754–95) was very detailed in its colouring. Von F.A. Kannegiesser, in his book *Aurikel Flora*, published in 1801, showed 66 life-size individual flowers with very good colours.

The green-edged auricula made its appearance early in the 18th century and nurserymen of the day showed great enthusiasm. These edged auriculas were a complete revelation on the auricula scene, soon to be followed by other previously unknown types, the grey- and white-edged. One of the first recorded green-edged was named 'Rule Arbiter'; the first white-edged was named 'Hortaine'. With this new material to hand, further selection was of the utmost importance, and by 1757 many became readily available for sale. Before the introduction of the green edge, auriculas had coped admirably through all weathers, but this elegant new addition needed protection from the weather if it was to be seen at its best. One hint of rain was enough to mar the perfection of its ring of paste.

There was soon no shortage of these edged varieties. Their names are evocative still – 'Grime's Privateer', 'Wrigley's Northern Hero', and a host of others. 'Taylor's Victory', a green, was proudly shown by a Joseph Partington of Middleton. Only 16 years old, he won the top prize, of 21 shillings. Joseph Partington was a famous grower of his time; he exhibited his auriculas for all of 71 years.

Another Lancashire grower, James Fitton, started his collection in 1746 at the tender age of 15. When he died, at the age of 86, his son continued in his father's footsteps, and was still cherishing his auriculas at the ripe old age of 80 in 1857.

The attraction of the rare unrivalled plants now available for exhibition meant that auricula shows were extremely well attended later in the 18th century. Societies in different areas laid down very strict rules, with each type placed in its appropriate group. No efforts were spared by rival growers, who displayed their plants in miniature lamplit 'theatres'. Many of these ornate 'theatres' had backgrounds of black velvet, with mirrors placed in position to show the flowers from every conceivable angle. Others had colourful painted backgrounds of mountain scenes. It is from these theatres that the term 'stage auriculas' comes.

As Sir Rowland Biffen pointed out in his book *The*

Auricula: 'The stage was something more than a quaint conceit; it was an admirable device not only for giving friends an opportunity to see exquisite flowers under good conditions but also to afford the more knowledgeable ones a chance of going over them point by point.'

Prize specimen plants were coveted and could sell for as much as one guinea (£1.05). The Lancashire weavers were prominent among the growers of the day. Not surprisingly, the edged auricula took most of the attention. The continuing pot culture of these fine green- and grey-edged plants may well have created a lack of interest in the original border-grown varieties, but, fortunately for us, this group remained popular garden plants. Many gardeners could not resist the temptation to grow them, because they were so adaptable to Britain's variable climate.

Attitudes during the late 18th and early 19th centuries were changing rapidly throughout horticulture generally. With the auricula the standards were laid down even more precisely. Each part of the flower had to conform to certain proportions.

Nurserymen continued to satisfy the demands of the growers. Isaac Emmerton, an early-19th-century London florist, listed over 90 varieties in 1816, but he was fully aware of many more being grown by northern nurserymen. There were probably about two hundred named cultivars available at that time, at prices ranging from 7s 6d (37½p) up to 2½ guineas (£2.62½) for new introductions. A number of nurserymen were making their mark, with their names attached to the plants they raised—'Grime's Privateer', 'Gorton's Champion of England', 'Barlow's King', 'Chilcott's King', 'Cluff's Defiance', 'Kenyon's Free Britain', 'Pollite's Highland Boy', 'Lee's Colonel Taylor', 'Forden's Fair Rosamund', 'Yates' Lord Collingwood', 'Buckley's Jolly Tar', 'Butterworth's Lord Hood', 'Hedges' Britannia', 'Metcalfe's Lancashire Hero', 'Popplewell's Conquest', and 'Redmond's Metropolitan'.

I find the soil mixture recommended by Isaac Emmerton almost beyond belief, but he obviously had great faith in it. The mix consisted of sugar, baker's scum, nightsoil, sand, yellow loam (preferably from molehills), and goose dung steeped in bullock's blood.

Auriculas were treasured too by growers in France and Holland. The collection grown by the monks of the Abbey of Tournai was very large indeed. An auricula stage displayed a good number of plants and the monks had 15 of them.

In the mid-19th century, auricula stages, with their intricately carved structures, were still popular. There was intense competition between growers. Transport presented problems in these times and it was common practice for each grower to exhibit one pair of plants. Considering that these were obviously the most perfect of specimens from each individual collection, the overall display must have been superb. Many villages in northern England held their shows in local public houses; in the south nurseries or private homes became the favourite meeting places. Prizes varied from 2 to 10 guineas (£2.10 to £10.50) at these southern venues, but were more modest in the north. The most practical and popular prize was a 'copper kettle'.

As we have seen, the high prices commanded by prize plants in the early 19th century must have kept them out of the reach of any but the wealthy. Nonetheless auriculas seem to have penetrated all sections of society. The Lancashire silk weavers continued to introduce many more varieties and coal miners also grew them.

The number of growers seems to have declined in the late 19th and early 20th centuries, although new varieties were still finding their way on to the lists of prominent growers.

Edged auriculas had enjoyed the lion's share of attention for a long period, but now the alpine group was moving into the limelight.

Mr Turner, of Slough, was extremely successful with raising both types and at long last the alpines were proved worthy of a place on the showbench. These brightly coloured flowers with their varying tones created a new challenge for growers and a wealth of colour for visitors. They have many attractions, not the least of which is the almost weather-resistant flower.

In the latter part of the 19th century James Douglas Sr worked tirelessly in England, not only breeding new varieties but spreading information on his subject. His collection was beyond compare, and seed from his plants was widely distributed.

2

AURICULA TYPES

Edged Auriculas

Most growers of auriculas have their own favourite type and this is very often quite simply the first one they ever became acquainted with. I have never forgotten the picture of 'Greensleeves' that started my own search for a green-edged auricula and have since met many people who long to grow the beautiful edged types. The problem is that, despite the considerable time these edged auriculas have been in existence, well over 200 years, they still remain relatively obscure. There have never been enough to go round. But modern techniques of propagation are beginning to remedy this situation.

Early illustrations of edged auriculas show them as having distinctly pointed petals. However, despite the shape, the 'green' edging was of the utmost importance, a highly desirable and completely unique characteristic. This characteristic is probably the result of a mutation, for the petal and leaf have identical textures. We do not know, though, when the mutation occurred.

Plants and seed must have travelled quite freely between the florists of England and France early in the 18th century. There were French florists describing green-edged flowers, some from seed originating in England, as early as 1732. This seed was from a variety called 'Marvel of the World'. One of the first green-edged auriculas named in England was 'Taylor's Victory', shown in 1746, and raised by its proud owner, Mr John Taylor. The description of this flower, with its blood-red body colour within the green edge, may make you wonder why this body colour later became much less desirable to the purist. 'Taylor's Victory' won considerable acclaim, as did the oldest known named green, 'Rule Arbiter'. Grey and white edges were also becoming prominent, particularly 'Hortaine', a notable white edge.

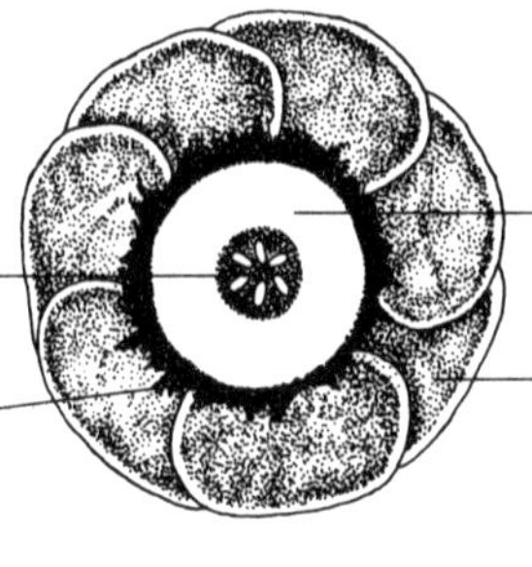

Edged auricula

These early edged varieties had characteristics that are rarely seen today, for, as well as being pointed, the green petals often had a light touch of meal on them. There was a great diversity of colours available. 'Oliver's Lovely Ann' was a bright green contrasting with purple; 'Page's Champion', another green, had a red body colour; and 'Lee's Colonel Taylor' had the coveted black body colour.

The edged varieties that have appeared in recent times have delighted very many visitors to the shows and fully merit the acclaim they have been given. But some of the older varieties still deserve a place in our affections. 'True Briton', a lovely white edge, was among the plants exhibited at the Crystal Palace in London in 1877. Obviously plants do not remain vigorous forever, but to preserve a piece of history like this is always a worthwhile challenge.

Another fine green show still seen today is 'Tinkerbell', raised by Clive Cookson in 1932. This is not an easy plant to cultivate, but it can be grown well and has won many awards in recent times. However, many experienced growers now maintaining this plant in their collections find it to be a most contrary plant. Although it has been rejuvenated through the use of meristem culture (modern science has now taken a hand), its flowers are by no means always identical. I regard this plant as a challenge and look forward to the day when it shows again the beautiful flower head for which it has been renowned in the past.

Many growers were making their contribution early in the 20th century, such as C. G. Haysom, whose namesake, a beautiful white edge, is now enjoyed by many and has proved itself to be a very strong and prolific grower. During a period of at least 30 years from the early 1930s onwards, Mr Haysom bred many fine edged varieties whose parentage may always remain a mystery.

One grey edge that I particularly like is 'George Rudd'. Named after a gardener friend of its raiser, this has been around since 1882. It has had its winning years and is often asked for even now. It is not a large plant, but compact and neat, and when other grey edges so often become more like whites, 'George Rudd' remains grey. It still offsets occasionally and will continue to thrive, providing pests are kept well at bay, for it has to be appreciated that a plant reaching this grand old age deserves an extra bit of attention.

Another fine grey is 'Jessica', which grows very strongly, has won its share of awards, and, no doubt, will go on for some time to come. 'Teem' is a splendid white-edged variety; it is a strong compact plant, usually growing at least two offsets a year. Many breeders use it as a seed parent. Its pollen was used to produce a very highly prized variety named 'Margaret Martin' which was first shown in 1973. This plant has gone through a period of being shy in producing offsets, but I feel it must be included here for its perfection of form, along with its new-found ability to offset much more freely. Surprisingly, a beautiful green edge, 'Roberto', also resulted from the use of 'Teem' as a parent and has become a firm favourite despite occasionally displaying a slight china edge on the petals.

It is always interesting to observe your own results when testing your skills at hybridizing and Mr Fred Buckley certainly proved his success when raising many of his edged varieties. Some varieties that began to be shown in the late 1950s are 'Chloe', which offsets quite freely, and 'Superb' and 'Greenheart', both of which are worth seeking out.

I have always had a particular liking for 'Lovebird', a grey edge originating in the mid-1930s. It has the distinctively serrated leaf shape that is an attractive characteristic of so many plants from the House of Douglas. Its stately appearance is enhanced by a neat and wholly attractive head of flower, and it is generous with its offsets. New varieties of edged shows are still being produced by notable British growers of today, such as Ed Picken, Peter Ward, and David Hadfield, to name but a few.

Fancy auriculas

A fancy auricula is one whose flower body colour is other than black.

Fancy auriculas, with their green, grey, or white edges, frequently display a red or maroon body colour and in the early days these were felt to be more acceptable than edged flowers with a yellow body colour. There was even a time in the early 20th century when the lighter-coloured selfs – mostly yellow and not highly regarded – were placed in this fancy section, but by 1913 if a yellow flower was rich and unshaded it was allowed back into the self class. We may wonder at the rigidity of these standards, which were so deeply ingrained within a proportion of growers.

Placing all these prejudices to one side, we can now enjoy the large collection of fancies raised by James Douglas Sr. He was extremely fond of these flowers with other colours in their petals, providing they conformed to all the other required standards. He had raised a large number which he felt were beautiful as well as curious, and encouraged many amateurs to grow them by offering his seed free of charge. At the same time he requested they looked for fancies among the resulting seedlings.

There are now many admirers of this fancy section who have a particular interest in these types and feel free to display them once more. It is also apparent that some of the eminent florists of the past retained their own fancy auriculas, such as 'Colonel Champneys', 1867, and 'Rolt's Fancy', 1894, which are still being grown today. So, too, are 'Splendour' (grey-edged with purple), 'Greta' (grey-edged with pink), and 'Fancy Free' (grey-edged with yellow). 'Greta' and the offspring from 'Fancy Free' are still with us. After World War II 'Rajah' (green-edged with scarlet), 'Victory' (green-edged with yellow), and 'Grey Monarch' (grey-edged with yellow) appeared on the scene. The list of known varieties is now considerable, with many desirable plants among them. Hopefully the renewed interest in and acceptance of these fancy auriculas will be maintained for many years to come.

Selfs

When I began to gather information about auriculas, I found that the classification of the different types was a subject that took time to understand fully. The term 'self', so readily understood by growers familiar with this plant, can appear confusing to a newcomer. The key is to look for that distinctive ring of paste within the singly coloured margin that is present in all the show selfs of today. Precise dates of their entry into auricula history cannot be verified, but it is safe to assume they were very much in evidence well over 200 years ago, in the favourite colours of that time. This tended to be the darker shades of purple, blue, and red and, in fact, almost black. With the continual sowing of seed which was the main source of new varieties, a large number displayed this dark colouring, which is not surprising if the seed originated from an edged variety with the black body colour. New seedlings from green edges have often grown into selfs, losing the green edging while maintaining the paste and body colour. This is well illustrated when red selfs show up in a batch of seedlings from green/red fancies.

It is strange how one or other type of auricula has at times been almost completely neglected, only to be grown in abundance a few years later. The selfs went through a popular period in the latter part of the 19th century, but then hit an all-time low for at least four decades early on in the 20th century, with very few being grown for exhibition during the greater part of this period. Fortunately, growers then began to take an interest in selfs again and many notable varieties re-appeared on the scene, along with new introductions. One legendary plant is 'Harrison Weir', a bright red self. It was introduced in 1908, and has since won numerous awards. It has all the desirable qualities of a show self, with pure, even colouring on its finely textured petals.

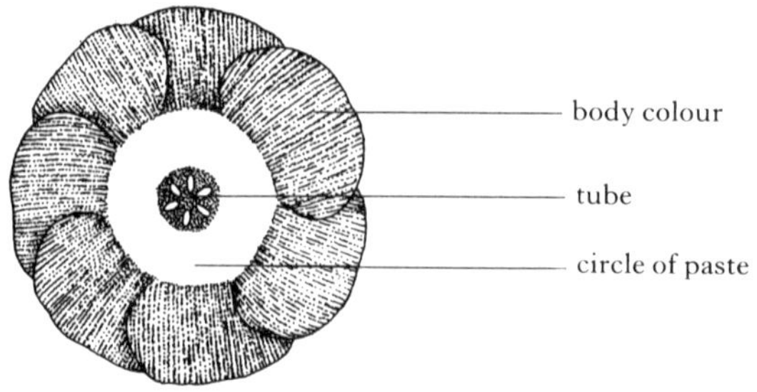

Self auricula

This was undoubtedly a hard plant to follow but selfs have always been raised with a concentration on one or other colour according to the fancy of the grower or the fashion at the time.

It is of course the coloured margins in their vast variety which can cause you to wonder if any two are alike. There are prolific blues such as 'Remus' and stately classic dark selfs like 'Mikado' and 'Neat and Tidy'. Pink selfs are represented with 'Rosebud', which possesses a soft, unique beauty. These varieties may vary in their availability but all can be obtained and all are well worth growing, particularly when you are starting a collection. 'Remus' is often so prolific that removal of its many offsets is necessary to allow its reserves of strength to become concentrated into its centre rosette. 'Neat and Tidy' is also no trouble to grow and will flower and offset very willingly.

The yellows are now grown in abundance and I always try to show a large proportion of these on my displays. They add the necessary brightness while at the same time creating a complete contrast with the darker shades. Some are of a purer shade than others. 'Sheila' is one of the lighter yellows. I find 'Chorister' one of the most prolific, closely followed by 'Brazil'.

A fairly new black self, a great favourite of mine, with beautiful blooms, is 'Hardy Amies'. These dark shades are quite startling, with their white paste centres; another well worth growing is 'Rosalind', which first appeared early this century.

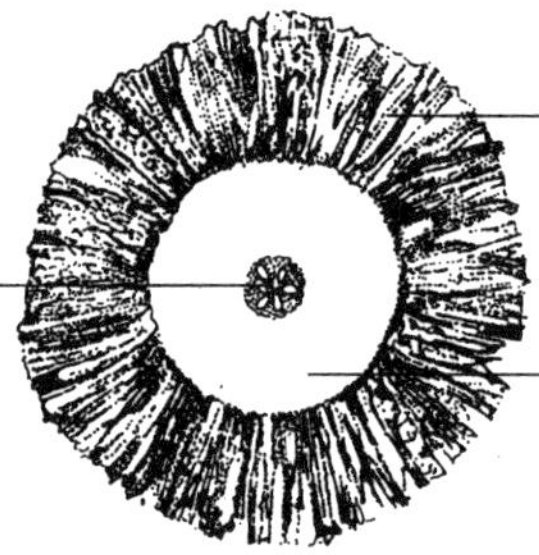

Striped auricula

Stripes

A striped auricula, purple and yellow, was described back in the 17th century and when I unexpectedly saw a very strong striped garden auricula – a really hardy specimen of this same colouring – I felt it very worthwhile to impress upon its owner how important it could prove to be. This plant had been growing in an old sink garden for well over 20 years, its origin a complete mystery. It has since become known as 'Kristen Stripe'. There is no trace of farina on this plant and it appears to bear little resemblance to the striped sorts painted in the mid-17th century by Alexander Marshall.

Striped auriculas were more widely listed later in the 17th century. A well-known British nurseryman, John Rea, listed two purple stripes. Later, after the nursery had been inherited by his daughter and her husband, his son-in-law, the Rev. Gilbert, listed a far larger number of auriculas, many of which were striped types.

This group was enjoying a period of popularity and commanding very high prices at this time. They were still in cultivation in the mid-18th century, when George Ehret, the famous plant illustrator, depicted four striped auriculas. Of these 'Glory of Chilton' had the most unusual colourings, with its yellow petals striped with brown. But after this these once-prized varieties apparently vanished from the scene.

It is in circumstances such as this, with the sad disappearance of these unique specimens, that the devotion of the true florist becomes apparent. Sir Rowland Biffen strove unceasingly to bring striped auriculas back on to the scene and his efforts eventually proved successful shortly before he died in 1949. The fate of his striped plants, though, is unknown and another few years elapsed, taking us to the early 1960s, before two more florists restored the striped oddities once more. Dr Cecil Jones of Llanelli in Wales noticed a show-edged variety, belonging to the Rev. Oscar Moreton, which had a definite appearance of striping within the flower. The Rev. Moreton kindly sent an offset from this plant to Dr Jones and the plant thrived during the next couple of years. At the same time, Dr Jones had heard of another plant noted for its striped appearance, 'Mrs. Dargan'. He bought the plant and now had in hand the material for a hybridizing programme. But, as a busy doctor, he was unable to continue the work, although he now looks forward to creating something new within the auricula family. His original auricula plants did not, however, go to waste. Mr Allan Hawkes was given the original plants by Dr Jones and started his own programme, painstakingly crossing and back-crossing, patiently awaiting the longed-for result. It took eight years for the desired striping to begin to appear, but appear it did and this type of auricula has virtually been re-created by Allan Hawkes alone. 'Kristen Stripe' intrigued him when first shown and he duly received its very first offset.

There are surely boundless possibilities for the striped auricula, which is obviously still in its very early days of development. These plants are a most unusual type of auricula and do not as yet multiply at great speed, but other growers are already attracted to them and in the fullness of time their availability will be improved. Their names are very appropriate – 'Mohawk Stripe', 'Rover Stripe', and 'Macbeth Stripe', to name but a few – and perhaps, in the not too distant future, there will be enough in circulation for other amateurs to share in this re-created pleasure.

Doubles

If you are a lover of double flowers, you will certainly find a wealth of variety in the double auriculas grown today. These plants were definitely grown by early enthusiasts, for we can see four of them illustrated in Alexander Marshall's mid-17th-century volume of paintings. They had a rarity value in these early times simply because they did not set seed easily. It is unfortunate that they were not more widely grown, for the few that were known about were

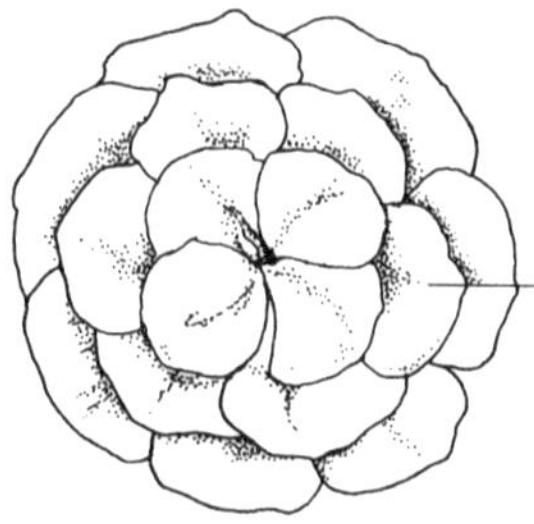

Double auricula

larger flowered than all other types, very vigorous, and had a most interesting feature – many of them were striped in appearance. This particular type, striped doubles, is something that I always felt would reappear – albeit slowly – on the scene, and rumour has it they are about again and worth looking out for in the future. However, in the early days the double auriculas virtually drifted off the scene with just the odd one reappearing in a batch of seedlings, perhaps the flower simply bearing the extra one or two petals.

John Rea wrote of a double yellow variety he was growing as early as 1665, but while there was, I am sure, a positive desire for these types to flourish and become more widely grown, the art of hybridizing, necessary for their continuity, was still unknown at that time.

Sir Rowland Biffen, well aware of the beauty that had existed within these doubles of a bygone age, tried very hard to re-create them. Although he had some success, it seems this was all too short-lived despite the many years he spent, his hopes rising with the results found in one batch of seedlings, only to go unrewarded in another. From Sir Rowland Biffen we can go forward a few years before another known attempt at their revival was made, this time by Dr Robert Newton. With his vast experience of hybridizing auriculas, he was only too well aware of the occasional seedling which produced extra petals. It is this awareness of the unusual which is always worth noting if you harbour ambitions of your own. Dr Newton already had three double auriculas in his collection with which to experiment and, by using some edged plants, he came up with a small number of doubles in a variety of colours. In due course, one of these, now named 'Marigold', made its debut. This is so multi-petalled it would be impossible to mistake, particularly with its colouring of a most unusual deep mustard shade.

In the United States of America, growers were making very valuable contributions towards the development of their own double flowers in order to produce a higher percentage of doubles in a wider variety of attractive colours. They have all displayed a dedication that has been largely responsible for the beautiful double flowers we can enjoy today. Ralph Balcom, Peter Klein, Mrs Denna Snuffer, Cyrus Happy, and Mrs Janet Round can each feel a justified pride in the new plants they have introduced. Plants were inevitably exchanged, grown on and continually hybridized, producing the many famous seed strains used by English growers to this day. English growers were inspired to create even more beautiful forms of this double flower, with the help of their American friends. Two of these English florists took on the challenge with great enthusiasm and the double auricula has now been revived on a very grand scale.

I enjoy exhibiting my double auriculas, for they certainly add to my displays of show and alpine varieties, helping to illustrate the many different forms that auriculas may take. They also tend to flower over a longer period than some, their many-petalled flowers taking far longer to open fully.

Alpines

Fortunately for us, given the system of classification used for the auricula, the difference between alpine and show types is easy to distinguish. The alpine group has of course a total lack of farina on flower and foliage, but it is nevertheless an extremely attractive section in its own right. There is a simple richness of colour within these alpines which is instantly eye-catching.

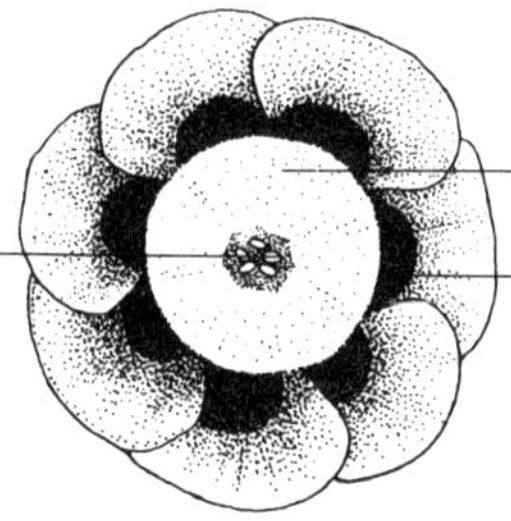

Alpine auricula

The one great advantage with the alpine auricula is its adaptability when planted in a border or perhaps a rockery. The velvety shaded flowers will not be spoilt when grown out in the open and their strong constitution is a natural safeguard in a varied climate. It is surprising on closer inspection to notice the many differences within this group. There are white, yellow, or gold centres, surrounded by petals varying from six to eight in number. The six-petalled flower is the one most commonly seen and, although these plants have been hybridized over a long period, I have yet to see a gold-centred alpine surrounded by blue or purple petals.

While the self is regarded as preferable if the petal colourings are of one tone, the alpine constantly appears in varying tones in many named varieties. 'Frank Crosland' shows this particular trait very strongly and is a very popular variety, with its light centre surrounded first by the dark blue, shading to a much lighter tone on its outer edge.

Within this group there is so much that appeals to the amateur and professional alike. The flowers are often larger in size than in other types. Ideally, the eye of the flower should not be too large, and should be surrounded by neatly flat petals. With the improvements made over many years, the petals of the alpine ideally overlap each other, producing an almost circular bloom.

The alpine auricula, with all its potential, has been through a period in which all interest was lost in its cultivation. For years the alpine struggled, while its edged cousins drew all the attention. Fortunately, in the mid-19th century, a Mr Turner turned his attentions towards the improvement of this group, aiming for larger flowering pips and richer flowering tones. His work proved so successful that others began to feel the same interest in this section. It was not long before growers started to raise many well-known varieties, some of which are still with us today. I have a plant of 'Sunrise'. An alpine variety of this name was listed in a catalogue of 1893 and priced at 2s 6d (12½p). It was described as 'large, deep, shaded crimson'. I shall look forward to my own plant flowering to see if it bears any resemblance to this antique, for it could well have changed its character over the years. One lesson I have learnt through many years of collecting auriculas is that variety names are sometimes duplicated many years on, which may lead to disappointment if you have been convinced that you have acquired a true relic. In the fullness of time all is revealed, for many auriculas certainly are long-lived and still extremely prolific. 'Argus' is one such; it is certainly one well worth including in your own collection with its 'dark plum colour, shading off to vinous red with a centre white and round'. This description, quoted from the Douglas catalogue of 1908, does this plant full justice, but today it would command rather more than its original asking price of 1s 6d (7½p).

I apologise for my constant reference to the Douglas collection but James Douglas Sr's contribution to alpines can scarcely be exaggerated. He carried on the work initiated by Mr Turner well before the turn of the century and his beautiful exhibits of auriculas were admired by thousands. His displays became legendary. Continuity was maintained when these displays were exhibited by his son and grandson in the years that followed. The outstanding show and alpine varieties raised by the Douglases over the years have been spread far and wide. Within the alpine group 'Bookham Firefly', 'Phyllis Douglas', and 'Gordon Douglas' are a few that come to mind.

The future of the alpine now looks very promising indeed; firm foundations have been laid and today's enthusiastic growers can show their plants with great pride.

Little needs to be changed in Sir Rowland Biffen's comments on alpine auriculas made over forty years ago:

> The Alpine Auriculas, although generally grown as border plants, can be made use of in other directions. Many find them valuable in the rock garden, whatever purists may say about their inclusion in it. The site chosen should not get the full glare of the midday sun, and if it is provided with underground irrigation the plants may be relied on to be flourishing when many of their real Alpine neighbours have disappeared. Failing this, the routine watering of the rock garden is all that is required. Another use for the Alpines, and one that will probably increase, is as decorative plants for conservatories and cool green-houses.

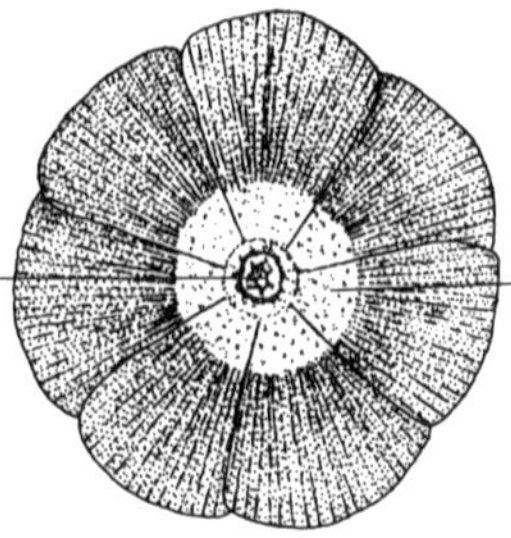

Border auricula

Nowadays vanishing incomes and labour and fuel difficulties make gardening problems a nightmare to many. If a green-house, stripped of its heating apparatus, can be kept in commission Alpine Auriculas can be grown in it to perfection with very little trouble.

Borders

I always associate border auriculas with those grown in such abundance in many a cottage garden. Very often a village will have many of one particular type, with a plant from long ago being handed out to its local admirers over a period of time. Border auriculas will be quite content growing outside in their multitude of colours, which are predominantly subdued – indeed, much of their charm is in this quieter tone. The soft colour is enhanced by a covering of meal on both foliage and flower, sometimes a light dusting, but very often more heavily pronounced. The rain inevitably has its effect on these mealy leaves, but they will always remain of a silvery sheen and none the less attractive. The flower generally has a slight dusting within the eye and this can also be very variable. There really is no set pattern, but many of these border auriculas are very true to the ones grown in the 16th century, which also thrived for many years growing in the open ground. If partial shade and good drainage are provided, they will prove extremely easy to manage during the height of summer and the extremes of winter. Their natural tendency progressively to lift themselves from the soil can easily be dealt with if the whole plant is divided, with each part then replanted up to and including the roots, which are generally found growing from the sides of the long carrot after a couple of years. In this way, the plants will then take on a new lease of life and give another few years of pleasure before this same treatment needs to be repeated.

There are many border types to choose from and I always feel the history attached to some of them adds much in the way of interest. The very early borders of the 16th century were akin to the 'Dusty Millers' we grow today and should easily be found in any nurseryman's plant list. 'Old Yellow Dusty Miller' has a thick coating of meal and in some years the leaves appear to be almost white. The flowers are quite sizeable and in this instance are certainly not subdued in any way. It has a larger flower than 'Old Red Dusty Miller', whose leaves are equally heavily coated and which bears flowers of a deepish red. Both of these have a very slight dusting of meal within the flower which adds to their attraction. Border auriculas are often heavily scented and these two are no exception, but this brings to mind another particularly heavily scented variety which is a paler yellow than 'Old Yellow Dusty Miller', with a green foliage contrasting well with its lighter flowering shade. This delightful plant is named 'George Edge'. 'Old Irish Scented' (see page 78) is another border variety with, as its name promises, a delightful fragrance.

'Old Irish Blue' is another border auricula well worth finding space for somewhere in the rockery or border. 'Broadwell Gold' is a fairly recent introduction, from the early 1950s. No doubt it had been growing for some time before being named. This bears large golden flowers which contrast well with its thickly mealed foliage. A favourite of mine is 'George Swinford's Leathercoat', which bears a small, delicate-looking, subdued pinkish bloom above attractive foliage. Despite its size and quiet colouring, it has always found many admirers when displayed. 'Blue Velvet' is another which will always brighten the flower border.

There is little doubt that the cultivation of border auriculas is now being taken more seriously. Apart from their obvious attractions, there is a tendency today to grow plants with a past. The preservation of these borders is well worthwhile. These are interesting plants, and, once they are in the care of a true flower lover, they will often respond with a renewed vigour, producing a stunning display of large blooms with each succeeding spring.

3

CULTIVATION

In the Garden

Auriculas have simple needs. Given good drainage in a semi-rich mineral soil and a yearly application of bonemeal, they will flourish outdoors in the garden. Despite its exotic appearance, the auricula has a strong constitution. It responds to commonsense treatment and plenty of good, clean, fresh air. In its natural habitat, it is protected during the long winter by a thick blanket of snow, which protects it also from the bitterest of winds. If you keep this in mind, you will appreciate that coddling is the last thing auriculas need. Frost does not kill them. Their capacity to emerge into spring each year with fresh young growth developing from their centre after the long months of dormancy can be startling.

I grow many of my plants in my garden and find their constant search for moisture and nourishment creates strong specimens. I have to protect my plants with cloches because I live in a region whose variable climate brings heavy rainfalls. Auriculas dislike wet feet, especially in a soil over-rich in humus – their leaves yellow, the whole plant seems to shrink, and they become victim to root rot. Apart from this one aversion, they are most adaptable plants, wholly intent on their own survival.

In the Greenhouse or Garden Frame

Most beginners, understandably, buy their plants when they are in flower and I will start my account of the year's work at this point.

If auriculas are to be happy in their new surroundings, their greenhouse must be shaded from the moment they arrive. They suffer obvious distress in extremely hot weather. The greenhouse must also be well ventilated – a continual supply of fresh air is essential to auriculas. If you have a cold frame, in a cool, fairly shaded spot in the garden, that will make an ideal home for the new plants. Leave the cover off unless rain is forecast.

By midsummer, when flowering is over, the plants will be ready for repotting. (I always start early in June.) The only plants that should be left undisturbed at this time are the seed-bearing ones, which should not be disturbed until their seed is gathered.

It is important to use the right compost for repotting. Through the years I have made changes to the mixture I use, experimenting along the way. Much depends on the materials available, but I have found this mixture to be satisfactory (all the measures are approximate):

2 gallons (9 litres) sterilized loam
1 gallon (4.5 litres) moss peat
$\frac{1}{2}$ gallon (2.25 litres) perlite or $\frac{1}{8}$–$\frac{1}{4}$ in (3–6 mm) grit
$\frac{1}{4}$ gallon (1 litre) silver sand
1 dessertspoonful (10 ml) slow-release fertilizer
1 dessertspoonful (10 ml) charcoal
1 dessertspoonful (10 ml) lime
1 dessertspoonful (10 ml) gamma dust

Make sure that the ingredients are thoroughly mixed. This compost will provide the plant with an ample supply of nourishment to last it through the next twelve months. The charcoal is added to preserve the 'sweetness' of the soil. The gamma dust is there to ward off vine weevils.

I use $3\frac{1}{2}$in (9cm) full-depth plastic pots for most of my fully grown plants, only occasionally using the 4in (10cm) size if the plant is exceptionally big. I have a high regard for clay pots but they are not readily available now. If you are lucky enough to have some, by all means use them – they have an advantage over plastic pots in that in a damp atmosphere they dry out more quickly.

It is much easier to handle a plant that is fairly dry. I begin the repotting operation by carefully removing all soil from the plant, using a bluntly pointed instrument. Root aphis is often found clinging to the roots at this time of year and repotting is an ideal opportunity to rid the plant of this persistent pest. I keep handy a deep dish containing a systemic insecticide. The whole plant – including the foliage – may be dipped into this then left to one side for a short time to dry off. This is also the time when many offsets – each with its own roots – will come away readily from the main plant and so it is a good time to add to your stock plants. These offsets, which will vary considerably in size, will be far happier in smaller pots. Their roots appreciate being confined while they are establishing themselves.

In their natural state, auriculas appear to lift themselves out of their surrounding soil. The same thing happens with pot-grown plants – fresh, vigorous roots appear from the root stock well above the surface of the soil. The removal of the lower part of the old carrot when repotting will enable these newer, healthier roots to have the necessary contact with the soil so that they can feed the plant more effectively.

Any wounds resulting from any of these procedures must now be treated generously with flowers of sulphur, to prevent fungal infection.

The actual repotting can now be carried out. Put crocks, large grit, or other drainage material in the pot before proceeding. Some experienced growers put zinc discs in the bottom of pots, to keep out worms which would disturb the roots. Repot carefully, but firmly, ensuring that the carrot shows just above the soil level. Planting too deeply can encourage rotting from the centre. I add a fertilizer when giving freshly potted plants their initial watering, to settle them in and give them a boost.

Freshly potted auriculas very much appreciate spending the next three to four months outside, in a shady position. The constant fresh air is beneficial to them. I like to place my plants in a cold frame on a mixture of gravel and sand. It is then easier to protect them from sudden downpours, which they like not at all. If the covers have to be kept on for long periods of time, using fairly shallow frames will avoid drawing up the foliage.

Of necessity, though, some of my plants are also kept in the greenhouse. Ventilation and shading is of the utmost importance and many methods can be used. I drape a fairly thick green mesh net completely over the roof area and leave windows and doors open at all times. In extremely hot weather, I place sheets of newspaper along the bench, completely covering all the plants until the evening. To moisten the atmosphere, I spray over the greenhouse flooring if extremely hot weather is forecast.

Auriculas need time to adjust to their new pots and compost. Their roots will not immediately and automatically function at full efficiency. You may find that the odd plant appears distressed. Should this happen for no obvious reason, remove the plant completely from its new home and inspect it carefully. Occasionally the culprit is rot above or below soil level that previously went undetected. Always cut any offending parts away cleanly and leave to dry out for a short period before dusting and repotting. I tend to go round my plants regularly, brushing the leaf in an upward direction with my fingers. If the leaf is firm to the touch, I feel confident that all is well.

Once the plants are established in their summer quarters, with all possible precautions taken, watering will be of the utmost importance, particularly in extremely hot spells. The plant has recently performed to its best, with all its efforts so far expended on its flowers, and it is now coming within reach of a well-earned rest. Drooping of the leaves in exceptionally hot spells does not mean that an instant soaking is necessary. In fact, very careful watering is advisable during the summer months. Large leaves form near the base of plants during this period, protecting and shading the all-important carrot.

For approximately four to six weeks freshly potted plants will not show much noticeable regrowth above soil level, but during late summer the roots will become extremely active and a marked re-growth will be apparent. Additional watering will then be needed. Never, though, water unnecessarily – touching the top soil will normally reveal whether it is completely dry or still holding moisture – and never presume that all the plants require watering at the same time. I like to use a can with a long, narrow spout to avoid splashing the leaves.

After this burst of new growth, late autumn brings shortened daylight and a much cooler atmosphere. Preparations must be made for the plant's winter rest.

Shading is unnecessary now, for the plants need to derive all benefit from any remaining sunshine.

Returning all plants to the greenhouse now will afford them added protection during the months ahead. It is not unusual for fresh flower trusses to appear at this time of year; they can either be enjoyed or, if you wish, nipped off to preserve the plant's resources for the spring. This reappearance of buds should reassure you that the plant is happily settled into the compost and that it will remain so until its yearly repotting is due.

Ensure now that no debris remains on the plants. The rosette needs to be completely clear of any remaining particle of old leaf or stalk. Tweezers are invaluable for this necessary task.

During the winter months the auricula goes through a semi-dormant period. The greenhouse ventilators should remain open throughout the winter to allow air circulation; they should be closed only during foggy weather. An alert eye must still be kept on the plants, because under glass they will soon dry out in winter sunshine. An early morning drink, which will be absorbed during the day, may be necessary. The plants will look very sorry for themselves during extremely frosty weather, but they will be quite safe if they are kept on the dry side.

As winter draws to an end, the auriculas will begin to put on growth. This can be a tricky time, with frost a constant possibility. Covering the plants with newspaper overnight is a simple and worthwhile precaution to prevent lasting damage to the developing buds.

For beginners, who are perhaps unsure of their ability to satisfy the needs of these newly acquired treasures through their first winter, the basic requirements are threefold only:

1 Ensure constant ventilation
2 Keep pots very dry, although not dust dry
3 Water only when absolutely necessary.

With the lengthening daylight, growth will become more apparent. I like then to give weekly feeds with a liquid fertilizer high in nitrogen.

Once again, the plants will need to be cleaned up considerably with the further removal of dead leaves. Most of these will be just above soil level and their removal will reveal the new offsets growing from the base of the plant.

I prefer to leave at least two to three offsets intact to enhance the appearance when the plants are used for my displays. When the plant is not for display, I remove the offsets after the plant has flowered, when it is quite safe to remove them. They can be removed by carefully and gently teasing them away from the main plant. They will often have roots attached and may be potted as described in the next chapter. It is advisable to make good the disturbed compost in the main pot, firming the soil back into place.

Some growers choose to top dress at this stage. I prefer to leave the top layer of soil intact as there are numerous roots just below soil level. However, the surface may appear solid, necessitating a light raking over allowing in air and generally freshening up the plant. This can be beneficial and should be followed by a light layer of fresh compost firmly placed on to the surface.

It is also at this time you may find that some plants have become rather loosely potted. They will need firming in their pots and perhaps some extra compost. Regular yearly top dressing was practised by a few many years ago but, bearing in mind that the fresh roots at the top end of the carrot, just below soil level, are the very roots upon which so much depends, I would advise against this practice. The compost should be rich enough to sustain the plant until the potting season begins. The only other minor but important task is the covering of any surface roots, many of which can begin to put in an appearance at this time of year.

I carry on with the weekly high-nitrogen feed until the flower trusses can just be seen emerging from deep within the plant. Then I change to a fertilizer high in potash.

Now, at long last, you are about to be rewarded with a beautiful display of flower and fragrance. Now, with each passing day, the new growth becomes more noticeable.

You must replace the shading material, to avoid distress and leaf burn. The warmer days mean that correct watering must be sustained, never leaving a plant either too dry or waterlogged. At the same time a constant circulation of fresh air must be maintained.

Now is the time to enjoy your flowers, each with its own beauty. Flower trusses, hidden one day, will appear the next. At the same time, you will be aware that the perfume from early flowers fills the greenhouse as you make your daily inspection. This wander into the greenhouse will not necessarily be a planned exercise. However busy your daily routine, you become drawn instinctively towards the greenhouse, making time to stand still for a few precious moments while you absorb the inimitable beauty of the auricula.

The alpines are usually the first to open, showing off their vibrant colours to the full. Once the buds begin to swell, the stem has usually reached its full height. With these earlier flowers coming into full bloom, it is advisable to remain aware that an unexpected frost may still occur. The simple precaution of covering with sheets of newspaper still holds good, with a few plant stakes some 12in (30cm) to 18in (45cm) high placed in pots at regular intervals to keep the paper well above flower level.

Although there is no set pattern, the selfs are usually the next to make their entrance, followed slightly later by the edged varieties, which will remain in pristine condition for two to three weeks. The doubles will start somewhere midway between the others; their petals unfold gradually, extending their flowering time.

While you admire your plants in flower, you must not forget to attend to their needs. You must be as careful as always about watering. At this stage a drink every other day is about right. Take great care not to splash the foliage. Position the pots on the greenhouse bench so that they all get their full share of light, and make sure that you leave enough room between the pots to make it easy to inspect them and to pick them up.

I always leave a shady spot free so that I can transfer to it plants coming into bloom too fast, but it is probably best that the beginner simply enjoys the beauty of the flowers, leaving the intricacies of forcing them forward or holding them back until he or she becomes more experienced. Some auriculas resent their flowering time being brought forward – if heat is used to bring the plant on it will only achieve weak, drawn growth with pale leaves and the vibrant flower colours will be faded.

Perhaps the best advice I can give about cultivation is 'don't let yourself become over-anxious'. The most important thing is simply to enjoy your auriculas. They are not difficult to grow well and through their beauty they will give you much pleasure. So take the time to stand and stare and to appreciate their qualities. In 1732 a British clergyman, translating from the French, wrote: 'The auricula has qualities over and above other flowers: it is green all the year round, and consequently the fancier has the joy of watching its development or checking its decadence: it has a fragrance sweet and charming: it makes very beautiful bouquets: it has constancy: and it flowers twice in the year.'

The auricula is also a hardy plant; it is a survivor. An elderly auricula fancier of my acquaintance told me this story. He was walking with friends in Epping Forest in the south of England when:

> quite suddenly we came to a clearing and I said 'There was a garden here once'. No sign remained of any building. As I slowly traced the faint outlines of a few garden paths a tiny glimmer of gold caught my eye. Full of curiosity, I gently parted the weeds and grasses and, to my astonishment, there was a beautiful little auricula alone in all that wilderness. We stayed quite a while and then walked on. Further on, we saw an old man leaning over a gate, smoking a pipe. We stopped to talk and I asked him about the 'garden without a house'. He knew it well, and he told me the name of the man who had once lived there. Not long after, in a second-hand bookshop, I bought a copy of the collected letters of that man. One letter, dated 1921, said 'My house in Epping has burnt down'. The writer, and the owner of the garden, was T. E. Lawrence, Lawrence of Arabia.

4

PROPAGATION

By offsets

Auriculas do not come true from seed, so until very recent times – when new methods of cloning became possible – their propagation depended entirely on the offsets provided by each parent plant.

When the annual repotting season comes round it gives you the opportunity to increase your stock. A plant that has produced a large number of offsets will have to be thinned in any case – too many offsets together in one pot inhibit the flowers and the crowding together of the leaves encourages rot. So, if they can be used for propagation, so much the better – in eighteen months to two years they will produce sturdy, flowering plants.

Small offsets that come away readily with their own roots already established are easy to deal with – they can be repotted immediately into a smaller pot.

Unrooted offsets have to be dealt with differently. I have used two methods for propagating, both of them easy, because at repotting time the plant is very active and eager to reproduce.

Method A

Make sure that you have to hand all the necessary materials – flowers of sulphur, a sharp knife, hormone rooting powder, a prepared pot of compost with an additional measure of sand, and enough plant labels.

I cut the offsets cleanly from the main carrot, carefully dusting the wounds with flowers of sulphur. The unrooted offsets are then dipped into hormone rooting powder and inserted firmly around the rim of the prepared pot. A $3\frac{1}{2}$in (9cm) pot will be

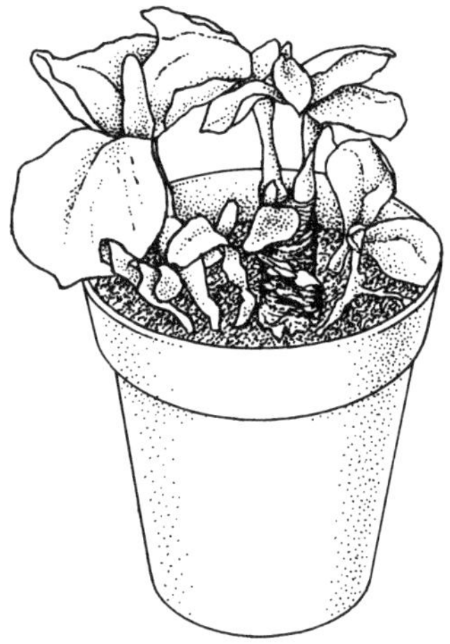

A plant with a number of overcrowded offsets, in need of thinning.

A plant after thinning, with plenty of air around it to discourage rot.

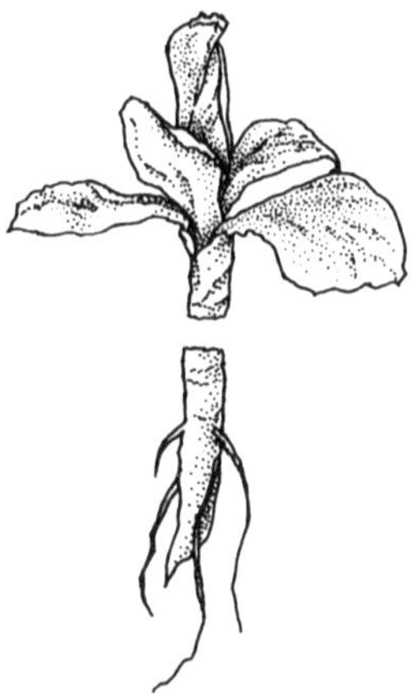

A 'shy' plant cut cleanly through the stem. The top part is treated as a cutting; from the truncated stem new offsets will grow.

A good offset ripe for removal.

Unrooted offsets planted firmly around the rim of a pot.

large enough to accommodate three or four offsets, depending on their size.

The pot is then given a good watering and covered so that it does not lose moisture. Many old-time growers used bell jars. Today clear plastic pot covers are available – they fit firmly and are ideal. Alternatively, a cold propagator may be used.

The pots should then be placed in a cool, shaded place. Lift the covers at frequent intervals to wipe away excess moisture gathered inside the lid. When you see new growth on the offsets the covers should be removed – this will normally be after about two weeks. The rooted offsets can then be safely potted into small individual pots and treated with the same care as the other plants.

Method B

Peat plugs that expand when soaked in water are used in this method. These offer several advantages. They are convenient to store before use; they are sterile; and they encourage rooting.

A standard-sized seed tray will comfortably accommodate 28 peat plugs at one time. Soak the tray in water for a short time, until the plugs expand to a height of about 1½in (4cm). Remove the tray from the water and allow it to drain freely, gently placing an empty tray on the surface and pressing down to squeeze out excess moisture. The plugs are now ready to receive the prepared offsets.

It is a good idea to insert the label into the plug before the offset, to avoid disturbance. Then plant the offset firmly in the centre of the plug, using your thumb and forefinger. Be positive – a loosely-planted offset wobbling in its peat will not be inclined to develop roots. The tray should then be covered with the propagator lid and given the same attention and inspection as advised for Method A.

It has been evident to me that auriculas grow away at a faster rate and are far happier if grown in a fairly restricted root situation. Their roots enjoy contact with the outer surface and the top growth is noticeably very healthy. This is rarely the case with an over-potted plant, whose roots have a long way to go before they make contact. Peat plugs provide this necessary contact very early on. Their effectiveness is very well illustrated when a medium-sized offset grows bigger and more vigorous than its mother plant. Where a plant offsets generously, I find that, using these plugs, I can, with care, take offsets from offsets.

Plugs also take up considerably less space than pots. And, because they can be crammed closely together, they retain moisture longer.

By seed

It is always interesting to raise your own auriculas from seed, whether you have bought some seed or collected your own.

Gathering Seed

Auricula seed begins to ripen from July onwards and the pods should be gathered just before they split open. They will turn from green to brown and get brittle over a period of time, so there is plenty of warning before they burst. Using scissors, I cut the stem just below the pods, leaving the long shaft of stem to dry of its own accord. The collected seed is then placed into seed packets, labelled to record the variety, and left for seven to ten days. It is then very easy to clean the seed before either storing or sowing.

Storage of Seed

If your seed is not to be sown immediately, it must be kept airtight in cool conditions. Put the cleaned seed into a packet, place the packet in an airtight plastic container and then leave it in the refrigerator or any other cool spot – not, though, in a freezer.

Sowing Times

There are many varying opinions on the correct times for sowing your seed. If you are a beginner, I recommend February as the ideal time. This is the time when the older plants re-awaken into growth and plants generally stir themselves into action. The seed, likewise, is also most responsive at this time. At this time of year, too, lengthening daylight and cool conditions combine to provide the conditions essential for good germination.

A prepared offset (*top*) ready to be planted in its peat plug and (*second down*) the offset firmly planted. A well-rooted offset (*third down*), ready for potting, and (*left*) a healthy offset growing on in its pot.

Sowing Methods

Seed compost is readily available and it is a matter of personal choice when deciding between the soil-less or loam-based types. I use a soil-less seed compost and fill the seed pan to just below the rim. I then water the compost before levelling it carefully and firmly.

Auricula seed is very small and can be easily buried, so take great care to sow thinly and evenly over the surface. An extremely light film of sand, applied through a very fine sieve, will be all the covering that the sown seeds need. This very thin layer of sand helps to anchor the seed as it uncurls, while at the same time letting through the daylight that is so essential. The container must never be allowed to dry out at any time.

I always cover the tray with fine net, held firmly by wrapping it round beneath the container, and stand the tray outside to benefit from all the air and light required for the germinating process. The net is very necessary as it protects against heavy rain and strong sunshine.

Seedlings will start to appear within two to three weeks and from this time on the covering should be removed, keeping the container in a fairly shaded position.

Auricula seed is notorious for its erratic behaviour and the seed tray should not be disposed of for at least two years. Full shade is only necessary after April, but continuous moisture is necessary throughout. Intermittent waterings with a fungicide will prevent 'damping off', for, although young seedlings are relatively tough, this is always a danger.

Pricking Out

Remove the seedlings as soon as they are large enough to handle. I like to prick them out into a seed pan containing my potting mixture. This will comfortably accommodate 24 seedlings. These young seedlings should have developed two to four leaves before they are pricked out. You may well be surprised to see how much root growth they have made, but it is this that makes their removal to more permanent quarters necessary. Great care must be taken not to damage the fine long roots when replanting. However, once replanted, they can remain in the tray until flowering time, which should be within the following 18 months. They will thrive very happily in this situation if given the same care and attention as the plants already potted.

When their flowering time has passed, they will be ready for their first potting and thereafter they should be treated in the normal way.

An Old Method

Auriculas, it cannot be too often repeated, are not demanding plants. As long ago as 1706 the simple rules were laid down for propagating from seed, in an English translation of a French manual, *Le Jardinier Solitaire*:

> We sow Auriculas in September, and to make them grow the surer you must have Baskets, fill'd with a Compound sort of Earth, viz., above a quarter of Kitchin Garden Earth well sifted, more than of Red Mould, and above a Third of that Mould more than of Mould mix'd with Cow-dung. You must be sure to let all these be well mingled together.
>
> This Mixture thus made, you fill the Baskets with it and tread it down when you have so done. Your Earth being by this means even'd, you make shallow and narrow Drills in it, and then sow your Seed there, which is exceeding small and must be as thin as possible. This done you cover it over with Earth gently with your hand.
>
> This plant delights naturally in fresh Ground, for which Reason, that you may make it grow the better, you must water it slightly as soon as sown, and then set the Baskets in the Shade, till such time as these Flowers are fit to transplant.
>
> This Seed, tho' extreamly small, is at least Six months before it peeps out of the Ground, and when it does, 't is seldom before the end of the following Spring. Sometimes, thro' a Caprice in Nature, it does not appear till the Second Year after; which tho' it should happen, you must not grow impatient, since it is odds but it will show itself at last.
>
> This Seed, thus sown in Baskets, will undergo the Winter without any danger.
>
> This way of propagating Auriculas will be a kind of Nursery for you....

5

BREEDING

When you are a newcomer to auricula growing, the main aim is their successful cultivation – it is satisfaction enough to see the flowers each spring and to realize that this beauty has been achieved through your own efforts. Although I have grown auriculas now for a good many years, the pure pleasure I feel at flowering time never diminishes. Nonetheless, the time may well come when this is not enough and you will want to try your hand at plant breeding.

It is only natural to start sowing some of your own seed, purely out of curiosity perhaps, despite the fact that the pollinating carried out by the bees gives you no control over parentage. Many growers venturing into the breeding of their plants start in this way. The next step may be to isolate groups of plants away from the main batch in the hope that the bees will go about their work within the chosen groups at the same time. This may well prove satisfactory to some extent, and certainly I personally prefer to group my auriculas together within their classes.

You may then venture into a little hand-pollinating. Study your plants first and learn their characteristics, decide what type of plant you are aiming to produce and choose your potential parents carefully. If, for instance, you feel a desire to improve on the selfs you already have, examine your plants critically before deciding which to use. (I have always been very attracted to the gold shades, which vary tremendously, so I would choose plants for their depth of colour, along with their good form, hoping to achieve in time a deeper shade.) Look for a small, round, neat tube and a clearly defined paste

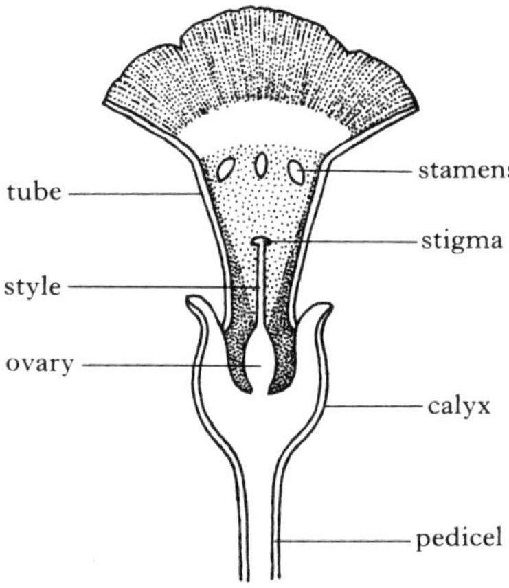

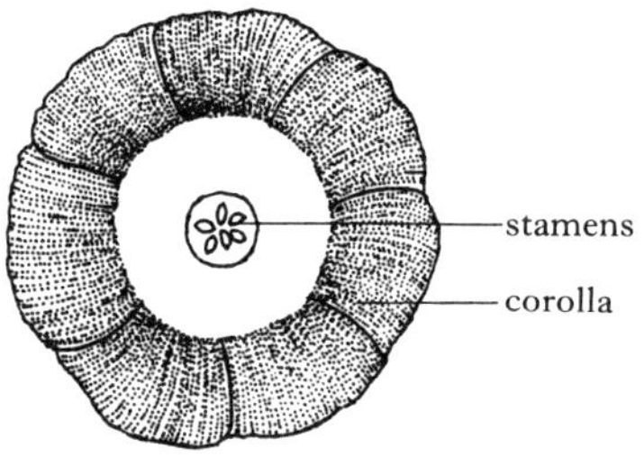

The reproductive parts of an auricula pip

circle. It would be pointless to use an ugly flower, with, for instance, breaks in the paste or a large, unsightly tube. Only time and experience can tell you which varieties to use, and you will inevitably have failures, but you have to experiment in this way if you are interested enough to want to raise new varieties from your own plants.

No elaborate equipment is required for hand-pollination. You will need only sharp scissors, surgical tweezers, and a fine camel-hair brush. The diagram (page 28) will make the procedure clear. Cut across the top of the flower on one plant to remove the stamens and leave the stigma free to receive the pollen from the other parent. If this method seems too intricate, the stamens from the first plant can be cleanly removed using tweezers. In either case, this delicate operation should be carried out on a half-open bud, while the pollen is still unripe, for it is at this time the stigma is at its most receptive. The stigma has a sticky surface which will hold the pollen grains immediately they have made contact. Using the camel-hair brush, transfer the pollen from one plant on to the stigma of the other. The ripe pollen is easy to identify – its powdery consistency makes it look like flour on the end of your brush. Sterilize the brush immediately after making the cross. The pollinated stigma can now be left to ripen in its own time. Mark a small label with the name of the second plant, attach it to the footstalk of the bud used on the first, and when, later, you collect the seed, you will have a record of the two plants used. While you still have these two plants at hand, it is advisable to reverse the whole operation with half-open buds from the second plant used in the same way. The buds open gradually and half-open buds will easily be found on both plants.

There are other variations upon this breeding technique. Some breeders prefer to handle the pollen without the use of a brush, holding the pollen-bearing anther with the tweezers and transferring it to the stigma in this way. Then again the whole plant bearing the pollen to be used may be held upside down, firmly of course, making sure the anthers rub against the exposed stigma of the plant below. It is very much a matter of personal choice and the ease with which you can cope with the whole process. You may have to be prepared to persevere. A disappointed would-be auricula breeder wrote this heart cry to Britain's National Auricula and Primula Society in 1951:

> . . . can you also tell me what to do to get show auricula crosses to 'take'. I've now got a few good named plants, and for two years I've followed all the instructions I can find. I've pollinated likely plants with camel hair brushes, twists of blotting paper, bristles from brushes, and cut off whole anthers and used them, morning, noon and evening, bright weather and dull. I've cut off the tops of the blooms to get at the pistil, and I've tried young flowers, middle-aged flowers and old ones. I've gone through all the stipulated motions and I just don't get any seed at all.

Despite this, the process in fact need not be lengthy or time-consuming. Usually much more time is spent in deciding which varieties to experiment with. So many characteristics which the experienced breeder has endeavoured to maintain in future stocks totally disappear, showing the desired characteristic – particularly striping – to be recessive.

Many breeders in the past kept no records. They relied on natural flair and an instinct to breed from the best plants they had at that time. Other breeders did keep records but they were never made public and have since been lost. This means that it may be impossible to trace the parentage of a particularly fine specimen. The lesson is – keep meticulous records.

Part of the fun in raising your own seed from specific crosses is in the anticipation. But do not be misled. Surely, you would think, two greens would produce a better green, two golds an improved gold, and so on. You would be wrong. Although you are shortening the odds against other colours appearing, they will still crop up. It is all a gamble. I hope, though, that you will persevere and that the successes you have with the raising of your own seed may lead you into the worthwhile art of hybridizing, for in this way the future of this beautiful flower will be assured for many years to come.

Do not be discouraged from experiments with breeding simply because you are an amateur with no special scientific knowledge. Between the 16th and the 19th centuries auricula breeding was all only a matter of chance. As Sir Rowland Biffen says: 'The breeders simply marked down a variety which they considered to be an improvement on any then being grown, harvested its seeds, and with these raised a new culture in which they hoped to find still better kinds. In this long period thousands of amateurs and professionals must have raised millions of plants . . .'.

6

Pests and Diseases

Although auriculas have strong constitutions, there are the inevitable pests and diseases that can cause problems if left unattended. The sooner they are dealt with the better, so a little time taken periodically to inspect your stock is time well spent.

Prevention, though, is better than cure, and it is a proven fact that the auricula is far more resistant to problems when treated as a hardy plant at all times. Other preventive measures are well worth taking as a matter of routine. I always use a systemic insecticide at fortnightly intervals to give my plants continual protection and I always have smoke pellets at hand to use if necessary.

Another point worth remembering is that auriculas, because of their rarity value up until recently, are often exchanged between growers. It is always sensible to isolate any newcomers obtained in this way until you have time to inspect them thoroughly. This precaution may prevent much trouble at a later date. It is an unfortunate fact that diseases can be spread and pests unwittingly passed around in this way.

Vine Weevil

This pest causes a great deal of damage if left unchecked. The first sign of its existence is generally a neat hole, looking almost as though it has been cut with scissors, at the edge of a leaf. This is a clear sign that the adult weevil is feeding. It hides during the day, often on the outer edge of a pot, and even if spotted can easily be mistaken for a harmless remnant of soil. If you find it on the pot side and knock it away, it will remain motionless and may mislead you into thinking it dead. It will however, quite suddenly begin to move and needs to be destroyed immediately.

The vine weevil has a hard, shell-like outer skin, dark grey in colour, covered with tiny yellow spots. It is about ½in (1.25cm) long. It feeds at night and lays large numbers of eggs on top of the soil. The resulting larvae work their way into the soil searching for food. They are fat, white, woodlice-shaped grubs with brown heads. Unfortunately they are very partial to all the parts of the auricula below soil level – roots, carrot, and even the young side shoots. If left unchecked they can chew right through the carrot and do so much damage that the rosette will fall limply to one side and the plant be beyond recovery. My defence against this pest in the greenhouse area and in my soil-mix is gamma dust, which is easily obtainable. For plants grown in the open, a generous dusting with a proprietary soil-pest control is effective. As an added protection, I routinely use a systemic insecticide.

When the plants are due for their repotting, keep a watchful eye open for these grubs, for if they are left unattended they will continue on their trail of destruction through the autumn and into winter, emerging as adults early in the following spring. I never rest easy if a plant shows little or no sign of the expected new growth from its centre rosette early in the year. The removal and thorough inspection of any such plant will soon reveal where the trouble lies. If the vine weevil grub is found, remove every particle of soil, destroying the grubs at the same time. If the remaining carrot is then sealed with a dusting of flowers of sulphur and repotted into fresh compost, it will have the chance to grow new roots and, hopefully, make a full recovery.

Strips of corrugated paper placed between rows of plants will often trap the adult weevils, which hide within the folds during the day. They can then be picked off and destroyed at a daily inspection.

Red Spider

This pest is difficult to detect; it is a tiny red mite too small to be seen with the naked eye. Its presence is usually revealed by a mottling of the leaves, for it multiplies rapidly and each mite feeds on the sap of the host leaf. This obviously weakens the plant considerably, apart from looking unsightly.

Red spider thrives in a hot, dry atmosphere, which is not a condition auriculas enjoy at any time. So if the plants can be left in a cool, shaded spot outdoors they will be much happier and the red spider will be very uncomfortable and will soon disappear.

The use of fumigant pellets at weekly intervals should remove the red spider from the greenhouse and there are many effective insecticide sprays.

Woolly Aphis

This pest attacks the roots and usually its presence is only detected when its attack is far advanced, when you may suddenly become aware of a woolly fluff around the neck of the auricula. It can be eradicated with systemic insecticide added to the water. If a first treatment is not effective, a second dose normally works. Some growers carefully remove the plant from its pot and brush over the visibly affected neck and roots with methylated spirits. It is essential to rid your plants of this pest for it will cause much damage to the roots if left unchecked.

Greenfly

These aphids are unfortunately very partial to the new young growth on the auriculas early in the spring. Because they are the same colour as the leaves, their presence may go undetected for a while. They are extremely harmful, for they can spread diseases on their travels from plant to plant, while at the same time distorting the leaves from which they feed. As the attractive farina-covered leaves of the auricula are so easily spoilt by drops of moisture, I prefer to use a small brush to wipe them off or resort to weekly fumigating pellets, rather than spray to eliminate them.

Sciarid Fly

This tiny black fly may appear quite harmless when first spotted hovering around your pot-grown plants, but it should not be ignored. The flies are extremely active during the daytime, laying large numbers of eggs on the soil. They seem to be more prevalent around plants growing in a humid atmosphere. Their larvae make their way into the soil and not only chew at the roots but also tunnel through the tissue of the main stem. An unhealthy, otherwise unexplained, discoloration of the leaves will reveal that they are at work. Liquid malathion at watering time will soon deal with the larvae below soil level and the regular use of smoke pellets will deter the adult fly.

Slugs

The succulent growth on the auriculas makes a very welcome meal for slugs, but scattering pellets, ashes, or grit around the plants should keep them safe.

Caterpillars

Caterpillars, too, enjoy the succulent growth on the auricula. They generally appear in early summer and can be extremely destructive. They can usually be sought out singly and destroyed. If they persist they will certainly succumb to the regular use of smoke pellets.

Botrytis

This is a fungus which thrives on plants kept in a damp atmosphere. It usually starts to appear late in the year, during the autumn and winter months. If the plant has been overwatered when approaching its dormant period, this moisture remains unused and can lie around on the odd dead leaf, producing the ideal conditions for this fungus to form. It is very obvious to the naked eye and, once spotted, must be dealt with at once. You may have to cut out the diseased parts with a sharp knife and apply flowers of sulphur to any open wounds. This disease should rarely occur if ventilation is maintained at all times and any decaying foliage regularly removed.

7

THE FUTURE

The wide variety of auriculas grown today demonstrates that this flower has already reached a stage in its development that could never have been dreamed of years ago. But auriculas still have vast potential and still hold many mysteries, and a single breakthrough may yet widen the existing range of plants by providing us with a new, so far unknown, type.

The recent dramatic revival of interest in auriculas has spurred many growers to embark upon the fascinating hobby of hybridizing. They hope to produce something new, by breeding from the best plants in their collections.

Most breeders cross plants from within the same group, hoping to develop the 'perfect' flower of its type. Others experiment with a wider choice of plants, hoping perhaps to see a greater variety of colour than the present combinations offer. It is a pure gamble, but whichever way your inclination takes you it is always fascinating to experiment. It is important, though, to keep meticulous records of your breeding programme.

An experiment with cross breeding may bring out a recessive character and produce something quite new. One experiment, made in the 1940s and described by Rowland Biffen in his book *The Auricula*, resulted in a plant with a paste that 'was of a pure sulphur-yellow colour' instead of the expected white. There is always the chance that a surprise of this sort awaits today's breeder.

One of my ambitions is to see a revival of the old burnt orange and sienna colours. Another is to produce a breed of later-flowering plants to extend the auricula's flowering period – where I live, in the southeast of England, the peak flowering time is the end of April.

But there are many different paths along which the auricula may travel. A recent introduction aroused a great deal of interest, for it was a grey-edged flower that had a distinct blue body colour – a combination that was both unusual and attractive. This discovery may have been the result of a lucky break or it may have been planned for, but its popularity was immediately evident. Some hybridists are aiming for white- and grey-edged varieties with greater vigour and still more perfect paste.

Perhaps the day may come when more pink selfs will be introduced. Most of the existing pinks were raised by Gordon Douglas between 1974 and 1980, but their numbers are few and growers constantly inquire after them.

Forms of double auriculas have become more varied in recent years. Breeding doubles involves intricate work – taking the pollen from a multi-petalled flower is a job requiring great care and dexterity. In Britain, Len Bailey is the leader in this field. Each year he seems to win awards with another addition to his multi-petalled 'Chiffon' varieties.

Also in Britain, Allan Hawkes has maintained his success with striped auriculas, but still looks for further improvement.

Undoubtedly we shall see new forms of auriculas in the future, for the possibilities are vast. Already one well-known grower is aiming at the production of a new double striped auricula. Another looks forward to seeing double greens, greys, or whites. Who knows what the future holds?

Colbury
Not many white-edged show auriculas remain today; one of the few is the beautiful 'Colbury', raised some time before 1960 and named after a village in England's New Forest.

C. G. Haysom

Raised in 1962, 'C. G. Haysom' has all the qualities required of an edged auricula, including an attractively serrated, mealed leaf. Because it is a sturdy, reliable plant that offsets freely, it is an ideal plant for a beginner.

Jessica

This white edge was first shown in 1954 and has since won several top awards. Its grower must be prepared to exercise patience and to give the plant some care, but will be rewarded with a show auricula of true quality.

True Briton
This white-edged show auricula is rather more than old established, it is a real antique–it was listed in Douglas's 1894–5 catalogue, where it was priced at 3s 6d (17.5p, 80 cents).

White Ensign
Like all the best edged varieties, 'White Ensign' displays not only a beautiful flower but a distinctive toothed, white-mealed leaf. Now widely distributed, it offsets freely.

Queen Bee
This exquisite fancy auricula was raised in 1984 and won a first prize when shown for the first time in London only two years later.

Salad
'Salad' (*left*) is a cross between 'Spring Meadows' and 'Ower' that seems to have inherited the best features of both its parents. It offsets steadily and is a fancy auricula that is well worth seeking out.

Redstart
'Redstart' (*above*), because of its entrancing colour combination, has been a consistently popular fancy ever since it was raised before 1962. It has won too many awards to enumerate and is always in demand.

Sweet Pastures
This fancy auricula (*left*), raised in 1963, has very large flowers which are displayed well above the attractively mealed foliage. Because it offsets generously, it should be readily available.

Beechen Green
'Beechen Green' (*left*) is a green-edged show auricula raised in 1970. Its name is a quotation from John Keats's poem 'Ode to a Nightingale': 'In some melodious plot/Of beechen green.'

Chloe
A very desirable green-edged show auricula, with outstanding flower colour, 'Chloe' (*right*) was raised in 1967. Among its many qualities is a willingness to reproduce.

Greenfield
A green-edged show auricula dating from the 1950s, 'Greenfield' (*left*) remains a vigorous, undemanding, and attractive variety.

Green Jacket
This green edge (*left*) showed true quality in its early life and, although it has now become rather erratic and something of a challenge to the grower, it is still capable of producing a lovely truss of flowers.

Greensleeves
This entrancing green-edged show auricula (*right*), raised in 1961, still grows strongly, multiplies readily, and is well worth seeking out.

Orb
'Orb' (*above*) is capable, in a good year, of producing a near-perfect flower. A green edge raised in 1971, it is now established, after a slow start, as a most desirable show variety.

Fleminghouse
This superb variety (*right*) can now lay claim to being the most highly prized of all the green-edged auriculas. Raised in 1967, it wins top awards with great regularity whenever it is exhibited. It is recognized to be a plant of great quality that always presents a balanced, well-rounded truss.

Roberto

'Roberto' (*left*) is a green edge of mixed green- and grey-edged parentage. Raised in the 1960s, it produces a flower truss of pure perfection.

Prague

A specimen plant of 'Prague' (*above*), produced in 1979, was exceptionally large and vigorous, but this green edge will always reward its grower with numerous beautiful pips showing well above healthy-looking foliage.

Superb
A strongly growing green edge, 'Superb' (*left*) was raised in 1962. It produces a fine truss of flowers, with each pip displaying a clean, bright green edge. It offsets steadily.

Haffner
'Haffner' (*below*) is now nearly ten years old. It has a heavy body colour and a well-shaped tube – attributes that fortunately tend to be passed on by its seed.

Broughton
One of the best of the fancy auriculas, 'Broughton' offsets adequately, if not generously, and regularly produces a fine truss of flowers year after year.

Idmiston
Another old reliable, 'Idmiston' is a fancy auricula whose attractive markings are always admired wherever it is exhibited. It has a strong constitution and an undemanding nature.

Rajah
The dramatic colour contrast so desirable in a fancy auricula shows supremely well in this variety, raised in the 1950s. It is an ideal plant for the beginner because it reproduces consistently and reliably and always produces a fine truss of flowers and attractively serrated leaves.

Rolt's Fancy
This venerable fancy is named after A. C. Rolt, the British commercial nurseryman who raised it as long ago as 1894. A good stayer, it won premier awards in 1927, 1929, and 1933.

Alice
'Alice' is a moderately vigorous double auricula that, when it was introduced in 1985, was immediately awarded a preliminary commendation by Britain's Royal Horticultural Society.

Catherine
This is a truly transatlantic hybrid. It was raised in the United Kingdom from plants grown from seed sent from the United States of America by Ralph Balcom, whose double auriculas had earned world-wide renown. It was introduced in 1961.

Maid Marion
Always a favourite of fanciers of double auriculas, the beautiful 'Maid Marion' is not a difficult plant to grow. It offsets unremarkably but regularly.

Marigold
A multi-petalled double that is unusual in form and colour, 'Marigold' is an old auricula that micropropagation has saved from being just a memory – so successfully that it has now been widely distributed.

Moonstone
The enchanting colour and superb form of this lovely lemon-yellow double auricula (*left*) have made it deservedly popular. It won a top British award as a seedling in 1978.

Hazelburn
A recent introduction, and a latecomer upon the auricula scene, 'Hazelburn' (*right*) is the result of consistent selection over the years. Its origins lie in the United States of America, with Ralph Balcom's breed of doubles.

Susannah
Breeders are always trying to extend the colour range of double auriculas and 'Susannah' (*left*) leads us into new, very attractive, pink-lavender shades.

Unnamed Double
So new that it is as yet unnamed, this (*right*) is a Barnhaven seedling that resulted from a recent selective breeding programme in England.

Grandby Stripe
The British grower Allan Hawkes is a pioneer and a leading force in re-creating today the striped auriculas that were familiar to our ancestors. 'Grandby Stripe' (*left*) was raised by him in about 1980.

Sturmey Stripe
Raised in 1975, 'Sturmey Stripe' (*right*) is, like all the Hawkes stripes, a strong grower that is prolific with offsets.

Tiger Bay
A more recent Hawkes introduction – it was raised in 1986 – 'Tiger Bay' (*below*) shares all the desirable qualities of 'Sturmey Stripe'.

Lechistan
A red self with dark, velvety flowers that contrast strikingly with the finely serrated leaves, 'Lechistan' (*above*) is a superb example of a modern show auricula.

Neat and Tidy
This deep red self (*top right*), raised in 1955, is a sturdy plant with a large flower truss held on a very strong stem. The heavily mealed leaves provide a vivid contrast with the dark flowers.

The Snods
This dark show self (*centre right*) was raised in the early 1960s. It takes its strange name from a tiny hamlet in the north of England.

Headdress
A show self raised in the mid-1970s, 'Headdress' (*left*) follows 'Geronimo' in being given a name with Amerindian connections.

Trudy
The red pips of this lovely show self (*bottom right*) are superbly set off by the smooth white leaves. It is from the same parentage as 'Gizabroon' (page 55).

Chorister
This unusually coloured self, first shown in 1967, is an ideal beginner's plant – it makes rapid growth and is prolific with offsets.

Elsinore
Introduced in 1976, 'Elsinore' has become an established favourite among show selfs. This is because, despite its delicate and elegant appearance, it is an unfussy, vigorous plant, easy to grow and easy to propagate.

Gleam
This well-proven yellow self was first catalogued in the late 1960s – when it was priced at 15s (75p, $1.75), half as much again as the other selfs in the same list. It has kept its form and is still a strong-growing, undemanding auricula.

Guinea
Another good choice for the beginner, because of its vigorous growth and reliable flowering, this bright yellow self was introduced in 1971.

Sheila
'Sheila' (*below*) introduced in 1961, has won many awards on the show bench. It is a show self with a gentle beauty enhanced by lightly mealed foliage. It tends to flower slightly later than most other selfs.

Harvest Moon
A favourite among yellow show selfs, 'Harvest Moon' (*right*) was introduced toward the end of the 1970s and has perhaps yet to realize its prize-winning potential.

Blue Nile
This blue self's rich colour (*left*) shows up well against its thickly meal-covered leaves. No more than an averagely strong grower, and needing some extra care if it is not to rot, it is perhaps not the easiest of selfs to grow.

Sailor Boy
Blue selfs always seem to draw attention at shows and 'Sailor Boy' (*below*) arouses more interest than most. It produces only a moderate number of offsets, but is not a difficult plant to raise.

Alicia
A light-centred alpine of most unusual colour, 'Alicia' (*left*) merits a place in any serious auricula collection.

Argus
Raised in 1887, and first shown in 1895, this light-centred alpine (*left*) has won a host of awards. Today, as a centenarian, it is still vigorous, still offsets prolifically, and still remains true to form.

Jeannie Telford
An extremely attractive and extremely prolific light-centred alpine, 'Jeannie Telford' (*right*) was raised in 1977.

Aga Khan
Another old variety that still has plenty of life in it, 'Aga Khan' is a gold-centred alpine that is certain to continue to do well on the show bench. A fine, sturdy plant, it is not difficult to grow.

Applecross
Already a top prizewinner, 'Applecross' is a gold-centred alpine with attractive red flowers. Micropropagation has made this a very vigorous auricula – when planted in a border it offsets particularly well.

Basuto
'Basuto' (*above*) was first listed in the 1960s, when it was described as 'a gold-centred alpine, beautifully shaded, with fine form'. The description remains accurate today.

Blossom
This well-loved gold-centred alpine variety (*right*), raised in 1960, won two top awards very early in its life – recognition that it had set new standards of excellence. It has remained consistent in form and in popularity ever since.

Bookham Firefly
Now well past its golden jubilee – it was introduced in 1936 – the gold-centred alpine 'Bookham Firefly' retains its brightness of colour, offsets readily, and still wins awards.

Doreen Stephens
The parents of this gold-centred alpine are 'Blossom' (page 65) and Andrea Julie'. The cross was made by one of Britain's most successful and distinguished breeders of alpine auriculas, Derek Telford.

Gee Cross
This gold-centred alpine is named after the place near Manchester, England, where in 1980 it was exhibited and placed first in its class.

Prince John
Raised in about 1916, this gold-centred alpine has throughout its long life been a firm favourite among both amateur and professional growers, partly because of its neat, circular outline. In spite of its age, it still offsets freely and it is still frequently exhibited.

Tarantella
A relative newcomer to the ranks of gold-centred alpines, 'Tarantella', raised in 1982, has the brightness of colour so sought after by growers today. It is now well distributed and will surely prove a future prizewinner.

Adrian
'Adrian', raised in 1970 by Britain's top alpine florist, Arthur Delbridge, has been widely exhibited and has consistently maintained its place as one of the favourite light-centred blue alpines. Fortunately, it is prolific enough to be raised and enjoyed by everyone.

Eve Guest
No doubt more will be seen of 'Eve Guest', a light-centred blue alpine of fairly recent introduction, when it has had time to become more widely circulated. It is a delightful auricula of much promise.

Hermia
An old-established light-centred alpine with out-of-the-ordinary colouring – it is a unique lavender-blue – 'Hermia' (*below*) is named after one of the lovers in *A Midsummer Night's Dream*.

Frank Crosland
With its beautiful flowers – deep blue centres shading to paler edges – 'Frank Crosland' (*right*) is a light-centred alpine auricula that has deservedly won many awards over the years since it was raised in about 1930.

Phyllis Douglas
Raised in 1908, this light-centred alpine is still worthy of a place in the garden today. It is sturdy and prolific and, in 1983, at a ripe old age, proved itself still capable of winning a top award.

Kingcup
'Kingcup' (*left*) has been regularly – and successfully – shown ever since its introduction in 1944. It is a sturdy and beautiful gold-centred alpine.

St Elmo
Another gold-centred alpine of great quality, 'St Elmo' (*right*), which has an appealing flower colour and a near-perfect form, was raised in 1973.

Merridale
Raised in 1977, 'Merridale' (*left*) is a gold-centred alpine that has retained its vigour and become a firm favourite over the years. It is the result of a cross between two well-known varieties, 'Goldfinch' and 'Overdale'.

Sirius
The unusual, attention-drawing flower colour of this gold-centred alpine (*right*) has made it a most sought-after variety. Fortunately, it offsets willingly and should become freely available. It was raised in 1979.

Gordon Douglas
This must be a strong candidate for the title of best of all light-centred alpines. Although over fifty years old (it was raised in 1938) it is still a must for the serious collector. In its lifetime it has won a phenomenal thirteen British premier awards. Each year it displays a proud truss of flowers and each year it produces a number of fine, crisp offsets.

C. W. Needham
'C. W. Needham' is an alpine that can always be relied on to produce a wealth of purplish-blue, light-centred flowers, of a beautiful velvety texture. Raised in 1939, it is now widely grown.

Valerie
An eye-catching light-centred alpine, 'Valerie' was raised in 1969, although not recorded, it seems, until 1972. It has since become familiar on alpine show benches, popular in part because it never seems to lose its form.

Vee Too
This light-centred alpine (*left*) was raised in 1973. It has many qualities – it quickly makes a large, strong plant, it presents a fine truss of flowers each spring, and it is generous with its offsets.

Dusty Miller
The border auricula 'Dusty Miller' (*below*) is so called because of its mealed foliage. The variety was common in British gardens at the end of the 18th century, but it fell out of fashion. Today there are many colour variations.

Purple Velvet
This comparatively new border variety, which has an outstandingly attractive and regular flower truss, is quickly establishing itself as one of the most popular and admired of all the border varieties.

Old Curiosity
Little is known about this attractive border variety; it is said to have been discovered in a cottage garden in the village of Houghton, near Carlisle, in the north of England. It is a neat, well-proportioned plant with an extremely sweet fragrance.

Old Irish Scented
This popular old border variety has been growing for many years in the gardens at Lissadel in Northern Ireland.

Paradise Yellow
A British artist and horticulturist, Sir Cedric Morris, used to spend his winters around the Mediterranean painting and collecting plants. On one such trip he found the border auricula 'Paradise Yellow' and brought it back to Britain to grow in his garden. The name, though, comes from the nursery in eastern England to which Sir Cedric passed on the plant in the late 1960s.

Old Irish Blue
A very old border auricula, of Irish origin, 'Old Irish Blue' was shown at the Chelsea Flower Show in London in the 1920s.

8

A Selection of Auriculas

Like every auricula lover I have my own personal favourites among the many varieties now available, but I have tried in the lists that follow not to be over-influenced by my own preferences but to recommend varieties that have undeniable qualities of beauty, health and vigour and are as suitable for the beginner grower as for the expert. This chapter should be read in conjunction with the colour pages 33 to 80; the two sections are complementary and together they provide a representative selection of the best of modern auriculas. The awards mentioned were all won at recognized shows held under the auspices of the British National Auricula and Primula Society.

Show Auriculas

Green-edged

Fleminghouse A favourite with exhibitors, 'Fleminghouse' yearly produces well-balanced flowers of a consistently high quality. It has been in constant demand now for more than twenty years.

Greenheart This sturdy, vigorous plant, which gained a premier award in 1967, is well worth growing; it multiplies steadily, while being capable of producing a fine flower truss each year.

Hew Dalrymple One great florist honoured another when the raiser, C. G. Haysom, named this beautiful auricula in 1947.

Tinkerbell Raised in 1932 (and in its early years known as 'Tinkers Bell'), this distinct variety has, through the help of micropropagation, become vigorous and plentiful. It presents something of a challenge to its grower, because offsets from it require a good deal of care and attention during their infancy. The flower truss can be variable, but at its best 'Tinkerbell' can surpass all other green-edged varieties.

Grey/white-edged

Ben Lawers A vigorous grey-edged variety, 'Ben Lawers' won its first top award in 1982. Its foliage is exceptionally attractive and its flowers are pure delight.

Ben Wyves This highly recommended variety grows strongly, reproduces steadily, and never fails to produce a sturdy truss of well-formed flowers.

The Bride Raised in 1959, 'The Bride' strikingly combines dense paste and intense body colour. One of its many attractions is that it has a slightly serrated leaf– often the sign of a superior auricula.

Brookfield This prolific and eye-catching variety has a smoothly dense paste and a pleasingly well-rounded tube.

Elegance This variety has unusually large leaves and is very attractively mealed. The number of pips may vary, but the plant is strong-growing and eye-catching.

James Arnott This white edge displays a beautiful flower matched with deeply serrated foliage that is so heavily mealed as to look almost unreal. It is easy to propagate and will reward its grower with many years of pleasure.

Lochnagar This elegant, long-standing variety, with its beautifully mealed foliage and smooth paste within its flower, is a great favourite of mine. It was raised by Gordon Douglas and exercised all his florist's patience – it showed obvious promise but for nine years refused to produce offsets. Fortunately for us, however, it has consistently produced them ever since.

Lovebird This is a very popular and readily available grey edge. Its history goes back to the early 1930s and it has won many awards, including two premiers. An ideal collector's plant, it multiplies readily and can be grown without difficulty to exhibition standard. Its leaves are beautifully serrated.

Margaret Martin When it was first shown, in 1973, this superb grey edge caused something of a sensation among auricula growers and exhibitors. It has been consistently successful at shows ever since, carrying off many top awards. It is a strong grower that multiplies readily.

Rosalie Edwards This beautiful grey edge, with its rounded, mealy foliage, was introduced in the 1960s and a particularly fine specimen was shown in 1969. It can take some time for an established plant of 'Rosalie Edwards' to produce offsets, but the wait is well worth while.

Saint Boswells 'Saint Boswells', introduced in 1975, soon became a popular grey edge. Easy to grow, it offsets regularly, and has now become widely distributed. Its attractive foliage is one of the qualities that made it top show grey edge in 1980.

Teem This fine auricula became one of the leading plants in its class soon after its introduction in 1957 and it has now won more prizes than any other grey edge. It is a strong, healthy plant that each year reliably produces offsets that ensure its continuity. It is inclined to flower a little late in the season and consistently produces a sturdy stem with five or six fine pips. Many growers rely upon it as a pollen parent in their hybridizing programmes.

Walhampton This white edge won a premier award in 1970. It is a healthy plant that consistently produces a fair but not exceptional number of offsets. The flower truss is held by a sturdy stem and seed is generously produced. 'Walhampton' tends to flower rather later than other show types and so it helps to prolong the flowering season.

Warwick Although only of fairly recent introduction – it was raised in 1976 – 'Warwick' is now fairly widely distributed and is beginning to win prizes. It has heavily serrated leaves.

Fancies

Astolat Raised in 1971, 'Astolat' is an example of the fancy auricula at its most refined and perfect. A well-mannered plant that produces readily, it won a premier award in 1976.

Fancy Free This beautiful plant has unhappily sunk into relative obscurity because of its grand old age. It was raised before 1934, in which year it won a premier award. Its descendants have inherited its good qualities along with the beauty of its blooms, with their grey edges and yellow ground colour. Many are proving a great success in shows and doubtless as more plants from this famous parent become distributed they will make an even greater impact.

Grey Monarch A fancy auricula of great charm, 'Grey Monarch' has a wide body colour of bright gold that contrasts with the grey of the well-defined edge. It reproduces steadily and is an altogether tolerant and amiable plant.

Hinton Fields Raised in 1967, 'Hinton Fields' was in fact a natural cross with 'Spring Meadows', with which it shares its colouring – green edging around a yellow body. It went on to win awards almost every time it was shown and will certainly remain a very desirable show auricula for many years to come.

Minley 'Minley' is an enchanting auricula whose beautiful green and magenta flowers stand erect above green serrated foliage. It reproduces readily by offsets, so there is never a shortage of plants for the beginner to grow. It was awarded a premier in 1982.

Spring Meadows This popular variety, with its crisp colouring of green edging around a yellow body, was raised in 1957. It still grows strongly today and reproduces well, with no decrease in vigour.

Wexland The large grey and yellow flowers and the strong, upright habit of growth of this fancy make it distinctive and desirable. Raised in 1970, it won a premier award in 1977. It offsets steadily.

Selfs

Barbarella A strong plant, with no vices, 'Barbarella' is a nearly black self whose dark colouring contrasts dramatically with the attractive foliage.

Blue Jean The well-proportioned pips of 'Blue Jean' have the most even colour and this, together with the exceptional colouring itself and the unusual length of the leaves, makes 'Blue Jean' stand out in my collection. It was first shown in 1972.

Brompton This brilliant yellow self shows smooth, rounded petals around a smooth ring of paste. The lightly mealed foliage, which is slightly serrated, completes the picture. Since it was raised, in 1976, 'Brompton' has continually produced offsets and consequently it is now widely available.

Cheyenne This is a fine red self made the more desirable by its attractively mealed foliage. Its flower truss is made up of numerous well-arranged pips and it is generous with its offsets.

Chorister This unusually deep yellow self, first shown in 1967, regularly bears a full, eye-catching truss of flowers. Few auriculas produce offsets as freely as does 'Chorister'. For its vigour, charm, and consistency I highly recommend it for any beginner's collection.

Consett Raised in 1973, this desirable dark self is capable of producing a particularly fine flower truss.

Everest Blue 'Everest Blue', with its violet-blue flower, is well worth growing for exhibition. Raised in 1959, it has all the qualities one could wish for in a show auricula – mealed foliage, sturdy growth, a steady production of offsets, and a resistance to rot.

Freda This stunning black self is, simply, unrivalled.

Lisa's Smile A pale yellow self, which is perhaps seen to best advantage against a background of dark selfs, 'Lisa's Smile' has a lovely form.

Melody Although this seedling has been grown since 1936 it has maintained its vigour and still regularly produces offsets to ensure its continuance. It is a beautiful pale yellow and shows a perfect ring of smooth paste within its flower. The leaves are attractively mealed.

Mikado This stately dark self has been popular for a great many years – the 11th edition of the *Encyclopaedia Britannica* lists it among the best auricula varieties cultivated in 1909. It had by then already, in 1906, been awarded a first class certificate and it has been regularly exhibited ever since. The fine truss of almost black pips contrasts well with the long green serrated leaves.

Moonglow Unusual in its colouring, and of exquisite, perfect shape, 'Moonglow' was raised in 1974.

Oakes Blue Introduced in 1974, 'Oakes Blue' is a plant of rare quality with its exceptional combination of colours – blue on a silver background – and its superb foliage – narrow, attractively meal-covered leaves.

Old Gold Raised in 1920, 'Old Gold' still enchants visitors to London's Chelsea Flower Show because of its glorious colouring. It offsets readily. Other gold selfs will soon be named and become available, so we shall soon see more varieties with this desirable colouring.

Pat For many years 'Harrison Weir' set the standard for red selfs – it was another of the varieties selected by *Britannica* as the best for 1909. Then, in 1966, 'Pat' flowered for the first time and was immediately hailed as the successor to 'Harrison Weir' and the brightest red of all. It has maintained its position as a top show variety for a number of years now.

Pot of Gold This fine, deep yellow self is aptly named – it has inherited from one of its seed parents, 'Chorister', the ability to produce offsets generously and freely, so it is easy to increase stocks and produce show plants of quality from the original plant.

Red Gauntlet The attractive yellow tinge of this variety's eye-catching foliage contrasts well with the bright scarlet flowers. It is a vigorous plant that is generous with its offsets. It was first shown in 1970, was voted the top self in 1976, and is still popular today.

Remus This readily available blue self will add an extra dimension of colour to any collection. It is one of the most prolific of all show varieties – it often becomes necessary to remove the offsets to allow the plant to grow to its full potential. The beautifully coloured flowers are supported on a sturdy stem well above the foliage, which is attractively mealed.

Rosebud There are very few pink show varieties available, but it is not its rarity but the beauty of its flower colouring and its leaf shape that makes 'Rosebud' worthy of a place in any collection. Introduced in 1975, it offsets at a reasonable rate. It is likely to hold its own even when the new rose-coloured seedlings now being raised become available, as they soon will.

Stella Blue selfs are always much sought after and 'Stella', introduced in 1966, is one of the most desirable – it attracts attention in any display.

Upton Belle This is a fine plant with large, well-formed, richly coloured yellow pips of excellent texture. It was raised in 1974.

Yellowhammer This beautiful yellow self meets all the required standards of excellence with its strong growth and fine colour. It was adjudged the best yellow when exhibited in 1978.

Striped Auriculas

Raleigh Stripe This variety has stripes of crimson, wine, or brown on a greenish-fawn background.

Tiger Bay Among the loveliest if not one of the most highly coloured of the stripes, 'Tiger Bay' displays fawn-coloured stripes against a bluish-mauve ground.

Virginia Belle This brightly coloured variety can perhaps best be described as a red self with a white stripe on each petal. It was raised, as its name records, in the United States of America – in gardens at an altitude of 3,000ft (900m) in the Blue Ridge mountains.

Double Auriculas

Catherine This beautiful double was raised in the early 1960s and first shown in 1965. It won a premier in 1970. It can be relied on to display consistently a fine truss of flowers. The pale lemon within the pip has a slight hint of green and is most attractive. 'Catherine' never disappoints its grower, will multiply cheerfully, and has proved itself to be a good seed parent.

Doublet This attractive form is easy to grow and to propagate. It will reward its grower with a fine flower truss each year and will provide plenty of offsets.

Mary 'Mary' was raised, like 'Catherine', in the early 1960s, from seed obtained from the United States of America – from the stock of Ralph Balcom of Seattle, who was renowned for his superb double auriculas. A gem among doubles, it won a premier in 1987 and looks set to remain a show prizewinner for many years to come. It has an excellent constitution and has proved to be a useful seed parent.

Sarah Lodge This was an exciting newcomer to the doubles scene in 1974. It bears a beautiful head of flowers with a truly classic form.

Alpine Auriculas

Andrea Julie Raised in 1972, 'Andrea Julie' has won two premier awards in its relatively short career and was placed third when the top six alpines were chosen for 1981. It is a plant of great quality and beauty.

Aurora This outstanding deep pink alpine was named after the Roman goddess of the dawn. Its qualities have won it many devotees.

Bolero It is to be hoped that this lovely alpine will soon become more easily obtainable than it is now, but meanwhile it is of such head-turning beauty that it is worth taking the trouble to seek it out.

C. F. Hill Raised by one noted florist, C. A. Hawkes, and named in honour of another, 'C. F.

Hill', with its glorious bright colouring, was introduced in 1973.

Elsie Introduced in 1977, 'Elsie' carries a large orange-gold flower which enhances any display.

Frank Faulkner This fine alpine caused something of a sensation because of its brilliant colouring when it was introduced in 1951 and it has since stood the test of time. Its centre is a rich gold. 'Frank Faulkner' has always remained a sturdy plant that produces offsets regularly.

Hillhouse A light-centred alpine introduced relatively recently and therefore not yet widely distributed, 'Hillhouse' has great beauty and potential.

Janie Hill A popular alpine since its introduction in 1961, 'Janie Hill' has received an award of merit and remains a beautiful addition to any alpine collection.

Joy Raised in 1931, 'Joy' has won many top awards and will no doubt continue to do so. Fortunately it offsets readily and is not hard to obtain.

Lady Daresbury This is a strong candidate for the accolade of best light-centred alpine of all. Now of respectable antiquity – it was introduced in 1932 – it has won numerous awards throughout its distinguished career. Not now, perhaps, as vigorous as it was, it still has a unique beauty.

Largo A gold-centred alpine of high quality, 'Largo', raised in the 1970s, is one of the top alpine prizewinners.

Lisa A joy to grow, with a beautiful flower and a sturdy, upright growth, the undemanding 'Lisa' was introduced in 1978.

Lyn This light-centred alpine became available only in 1981 and will take some time to circulate widely, but it is already being sought out by the more adventurous growers and it has already won a premier award.

Margaret Faulkner This purple-flowered variety, raised in 1961, seems not only to maintain its status as one of the best light-centred alpines but also to improve with time. It has been awarded several premiers. Still highly regarded, it is well worth seeking out.

Mark This is a brilliant plant, much in demand, and fortunately very prolific, so that it has now been circulated in large numbers. It has a distinguished parentage, 'Thetis' × 'Rowena', so it is perhaps not surprising that it won the seedling class in 1972. It was also voted the best of the top six alpines in 1981.

May Roberts 'May Roberts' is a large gold-centred alpine with a rich red flower that at its best can be outstanding. Raised in 1975, it reproduces at a fairly average rate and is always a pleasure to grow.

Milkmaid This easy-to-grow blue alpine dates from before 1931. Its well-defined shading adds to its attraction.

Mink A very attractive, brightly coloured seedling, 'Mink' multiplies readily and is another variety suitable for the beginner.

Peggy This richly coloured variety, with its reliably well-furnished truss of flowers, is particularly useful because it flowers slightly earlier than most alpines and so is conveniently ready for early spring shows.

Pink Lady One of the most rewarding alpines to grow, 'Pink Lady' always produces a large flower truss in a beautiful shade of pink. It has proved its worth over the years since its introduction before World War II.

Pippin 'Pippin', with its rich pink colouring, makes a strong, sturdy plant that multiplies quite happily. It has perhaps not been much exhibited in recent years, but it deserves to be distributed more widely and shown more frequently – I am sure it would still be in the running to gain many an honour.

Rabley Heath Raised in 1972, 'Rabley Heath' is still a sturdy and desirable variety that looks set to maintain its popularity for many years yet.

Radiant 'Radiant' stands out uniquely in any display because of the unusual shade of gold on the outer edges of its petals. It dates to before 1935, but it goes on reproducing strongly and none of its qualities have deteriorated over the years.

Roxburgh 'Roxburgh', with its clear blue flowers, has now been around for about seventy years but, although it may not be as prolific now as it was in its youth, it is still one of the great alpine varieties and is still well worth growing.

Salome Many plants have been named after Herod's daughter in the biblical story. The auricula that bears her name is a superb red-flowered gold-centred alpine.

Sandra 'Sandra', adjudged the premier alpine in 1982, is a superior auricula of a very refined and dainty habit. It has immaculately shaped pips and well-rounded tubes within which the anthers are neatly and prettily placed.

Sandwood Bay This brightly red-coloured gold-centred alpine has been consistently popular since its introduction in 1971; it has won one premier award.

Walton Without doubt my favourite among the blue alpines, this was a great favourite also of its raiser, Gordon Douglas, from the moment he first saw it as a seedling in bloom in 1957. The colour is striking – there is a slightly violet tinge within the blue. Happily, too, it is a consistently vigorous and good-natured plant.

Winifred One of the finest of modern gold-centred alpines, 'Winifred' is a vigorous plant that carries a finely proportioned flower truss. Raised in 1970, it always seems to feature in lists of 'top alpines' and is regularly named the leading gold-centred alpine.

Border Auriculas

McWatt's Blue 'McWatt's Blue' is a superb, richly scented auricula which bears dark bluish-mauve flowers with a thin line of light mauve at their edges. Its leaves are very heavily mealed and have a slightly greyish tinge.

Old Irish Scented The name tells most of it – it came from Ireland and is scented. It has also dusky yellow flowers with rounded centres.

Osborne Green This variety was found over a hundred years ago growing in an old cottage garden in Ireland; it is named after Mr Osborne, the owner of the cottage. The flowers have a creamy white centre with a purple body and a green edge.

9

GUIDELINES FOR EXHIBITORS

Show Auriculas

All show varieties have flowers that have a circle of paste, often called the meal or the farina, surrounding the tube that encloses the reproductive organs. It is this meal that uniquely distinguishes the show varieties. There are five different types of show auriculas – green-edged, grey-edged, white-edged, fancy, and self.

Green-edged

The auricula with the green edge has always been highly cherished by the few and desired by many. Green-edged auriculas were first recorded in the middle of the 18th century and since then have been painstakingly developed to today's high standards. The green-edged auricula differs from the other show varieties in that its leaves are completely devoid of meal. The flower itself is very striking, with its combination of rounded tube, white ring of paste, and black body colour all within the green edge. It is an apparent weakness for this flower to have a slight edging of meal, but when this does occur it is generally described as 'china-edged'. The beauty of the green-edged flowers becomes more pronounced when they open fully and become completely flat. They are usually the latest to flower and may go well into June before they are fully open. This process can be greatly helped along if they have a long period of bright light and a moist atmosphere.

Grey-edged

The grey-edged auricula has its own unique beauty, with a light dusting of meal on the edge of its flowers. It is this light covering in varying degrees which enhances its appeal. This meal may be on the outer edge of the petals alone, while the leaves remain a pure clear green, or a light dusting of meal may be evident on the leaves as well.

White-edged

The meal on the petals of white-edged show auriculas is so pronounced and thick that you could be forgiven for thinking it unreal. The contrast of this outer edge with the body colour, which should be black, is really superb. The leaves are often very heavily coated also, but some plants that come into this class have leaves almost free of meal.

Fancy

The fancy auricula adds a great deal of interest to this group. The outer edge will be green, grey, or white. The central disc has its paste centre, but the body colour may be anything other than black. The hybridizing that must have taken place years ago has left us a legacy of pure delight. Colour combinations abound and are far too numerous to describe. I generally group my auriculas together in each greenhouse and the colouring from these fancies is absolutely stunning in the spring. Imagine some of the possible combinations – violet with grey, scarlet with green, yellow with grey or white, and so on, with no two varieties exactly alike.

Self

This type of auricula is very distinct from other show varieties, for the centre circle of paste is

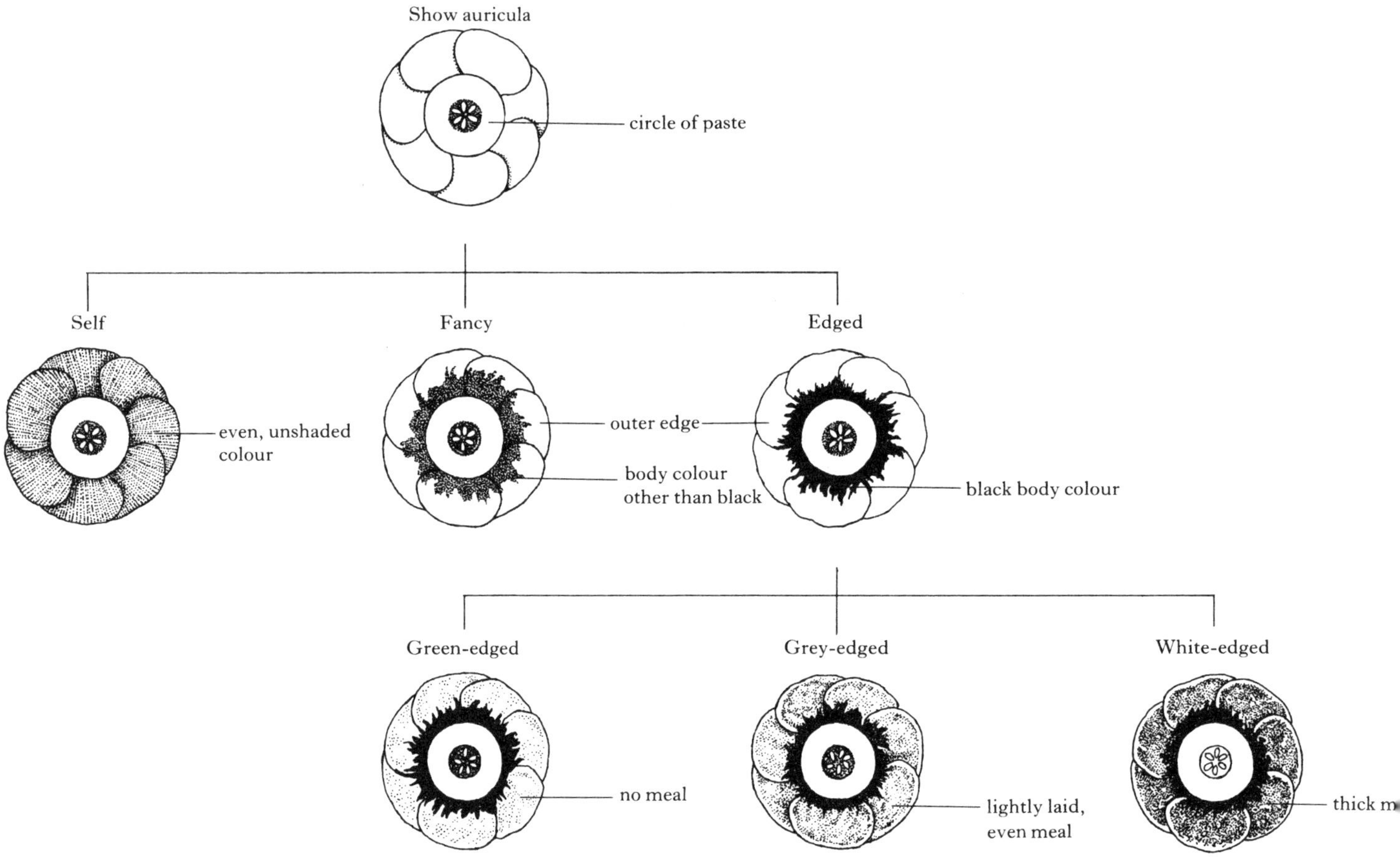

Classification of Show Auriculas

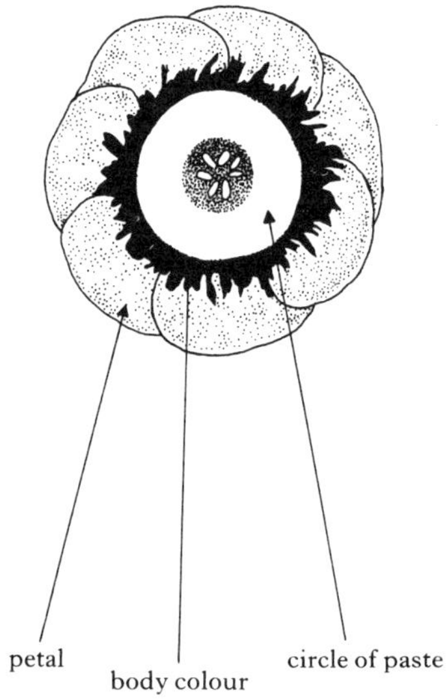

The parts of a show pip

surrounded by an edge of one colour only. This colour should ideally be pure and clear, without a hint of meal on this outer edge. Selfs have a delicately velvet appearance that belies their tough nature. The amount of meal on their leaves varies considerably, some appearing completely white while a few have no trace at all. It is the clarity, though, of the flower colourings that makes the selfs unique. Where else would you see a clear and pure black flower vividly contrasting with its white circle of paste, or other colours from reds, purples, golds, pinks, yellows, and blues?

Alpine Auriculas

The alpine auricula is very easy to distinguish from the show auricula, for its foliage and flowers are completely devoid of 'meal'. The flowers are often larger than those of the show types.

Alpine auriculas are sub-divided into two groups – they are either gold-centred or light-centred.

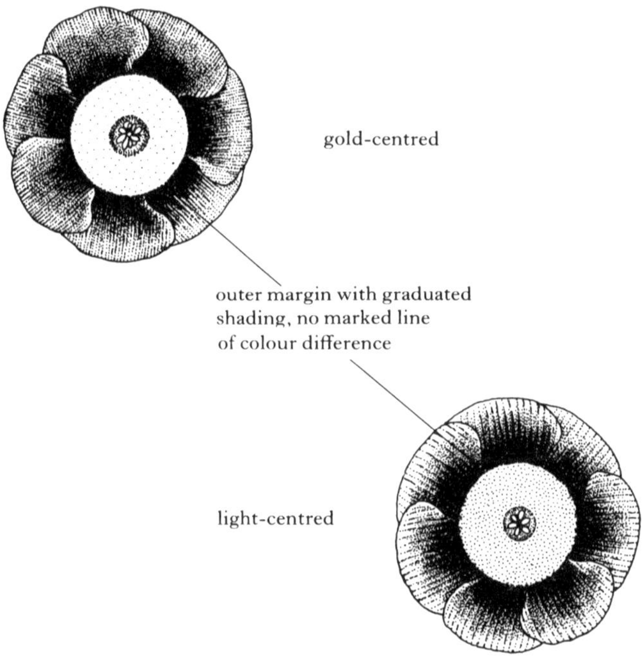

The two groups of alpine auriculas

It is the centre eye of the flower that determines to which group the plant belongs. The centre colours vary from white, through cream, to an almost sulphur yellow. Alpines were in fact divided into three groups in the early 20th century but the standards required today appear to favour the two-group system. You will soon recognize the alpine auricula and no doubt become equally enchanted by its clear-cut beauty.

It is worthwhile to group your plants into their classes when they begin to flower, for in this way you can then compare their differences and decide which plant is preferable in colour, shape, and form. For this you will need to know something of the standards by which the plants should be judged and you will need to have some knowledge of their characteristics and parts.

Meal

Looking back to the ancestors of our plants, we know that *Primula auricula* growing in the wild possessed mealy foliage. This is a striking feature, found in no other plant, and its development to perfection increases the worth of any show auricula. The meal on the flower can determine the degree of beauty in each individual plant. To see a perfectly smooth ring of paste is extremely desirable. This meal creates a unique beauty and even without the flower I can happily look at my many different varieties and continually marvel at their foliage alone. On some leaves this meal takes on the appearance of frost, on others it seems completely smooth. The amount of meal varies. A thin layer will give a soft tint to the foliage, slightly more creates an ultramarine hue, and when a heavier layer develops the green leaf can become completely disguised. This meal can also look extremely attractive when it covers the stalk and much of the flower – though not of course, the coloured portion.

Form

Every plant has its own distinct character. One may have a very short stem, another's may look too thin for the weight of flower truss. Leaves also vary considerably, some inclining to curl while others unfold willingly and grow very sizeable.

Some features are desirable, others not. The leaves on some plants can appear a bit untidy in habit and the well-proportioned plant with neat rosettes is always to be preferred. The stem held erect above the foliage needs to be sturdy enough to bear the weight of the flower truss. As the flowers open you will begin to judge their appearance. Are they too bunched and crowded, with too many buds? With fewer buds, each will have room to open, with each flower just touching its neighbour. Then the fully open truss will create a lovely rounded head of flower of which you may be justly proud.

It is time now to turn our attention to the parts that make up the flower itself, taking the show auricula first.

Parts of the Flower in Show Auriculas

The Tube

The tube is placed at the very centre of the flower and should be pure yellow in colour and circular in shape. The reproductive parts of the flower are accommodated within this tube and it is the positioning of these reproductive parts that decides the value of the plant for exhibition or otherwise.

The pollen-bearing stamens that are grouped within the tube look very attractive when formed in a

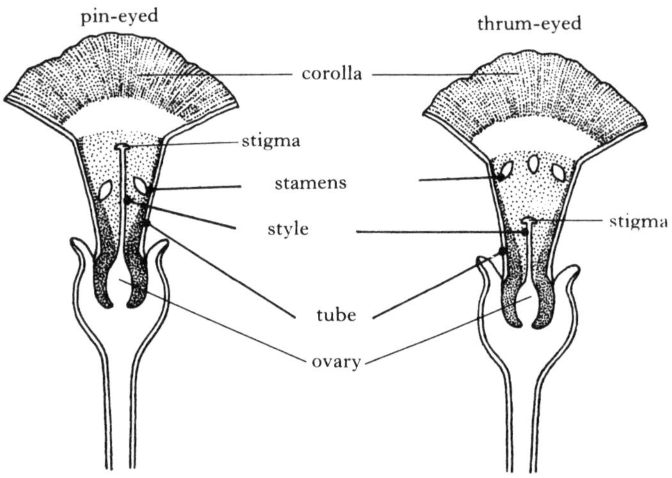

The two kinds of show pip

ringed shape at the top of the tube. This is all important for the amateur showing a plant for the first time, as the stigma is regarded as unsightly if it protrudes above these stamens, and an ideal flower has the stigma tucked well down within the tube.

The Eye

This is the white farina-covered disc. A close inspection may reveal blemishes in the inner circle of paste. Ideally, it should be consistent, with its meal pure white, thickly laid, and of smooth appearance. The outer edge of this ring is even more attractive if it does not run into the body colour; in fact it should remain within a clearly defined line.

Body Colour

This contrasts intensely with the paste, particularly if it is a pure black tone radiating out evenly into the green, grey, or white outer edge. The black body colour of the edged varieties was at one time the only colour thought acceptable and even today the purist disregards the fancy flowers with their varying body colours. However, there are now many fancy plants with body colours of almost every shade imaginable.

The Edge

A green edge with a freshly painted appearance is a rarity indeed, although it will always remain the ideal. If you raise a plant which bears a resemblance to this description, you could well own a real treasure. They are often termed 'Painted Ladies'. The grey edge is very similar to the green if left out in the rain, but when it is protected the light filmy covering of meal alters its appearance drastically. To aim for an even covering of this finely laid farina within your own seedlings can be time well spent. The white edge should also have an evenly distributed farina, but it should be dense and smooth over the whole part of the flower's edge. Unsightly, cracking, or lumpy meal will mar the appearance considerably. The self auricula should have an edging of one pure colour with no trace of meal at all. This colouring is held in higher esteem if it is one pure shade showing no variation of tone.

To give a guide to the qualities looked for in the alpine auricula, I have divided the flower once again into its parts. It is important, though, not to overlook the appearance of the whole pip. In the alpine, this should open fully to become flat and smoothly circular. The occasional flower has a tendency to remain cupped, but this would be considered a fault. The rounded look of the pip, brought about by one petal overlapping another, is a most desirable feature. Ideally, the shading should be gradual, becoming lighter at the petal's outer edge.

Parts of the Flower in Alpine Auriculas

The Tube

The central tube should be neat and circular, with its upper edge level with the opened flower rather than above it. The anthers should fit well into this upper edge and be separate from each other while combining to present a neat and shapely appearance.

The Centre

This central area with its complete absence of meal will vary in colour from white through to cream until we find some of the deepest of yellows. The perfect centre would have a clearly defined outer edge showing none of the slits that can occasionally appear.

The Edge

There are many attractive variations on this outer portion and ideally they should be of rich colouring, shading lightly towards the outer edge. The added flatness of the flower will improve the effect.

Societies

Denmark
Dansk Primula Klub: Ove Leth-Møller, Danmarksvej 41B, 2800 Lyngby

United Kingdom
National Auricula and Primula Society
Northern Section: D. G. Hadfield (Hon. Secretary), 146 Queens Road, Cheadle Hulme, Cheadle, Cheshire SK8 5HY
Midland and West Section: Mrs G. Baker (Editor), 19 Birches Barn Avenue, Wolverhampton, West Midlands WV3 7BT
Southern Section: L. E. Wigley (Hon. Secretary), 67 Warnham Court Road, Carshalton Beeches, Surrey

United States of America
American Primrose, Auricula and Primula Society: Brian Skidmore (Secretary), 6730 West Mercer Way, Mercer Island, Washington 98040

Gardens to Visit

Belgium
M. Fouarge, 267c Rue d'Ombret, B–4133 Clermont
J. Lebeau, 1 Rue du Vert Logis, B6101 Jamioulx

Canada
The Butchart Gardens, 800 Benevenuto Boulevard, Brentwood Bay, Victoria, British Columbia
Devonian Botanic Garden, University of Alberta, Edmonton, Alberta
John Kerridge, 246 West 47th Avenue, Vancouver, British Columbia

United Kingdom
Broughton Castle, Broughton, nr Banbury, Oxfordshire
Chatsworth House, Chatsworth, nr Bakewell, Derbyshire
Chelsea Physic Garden, 66 Royal Hospital Road, London SW3
Hampton Court Palace Gardens, Hampton Court, Greater London
Harlow Car Gardens (Northern Horticultural Society), Crag Lane, Harrogate, North Yorkshire
Hatfield House, Hatfield, Hertfordshire
Hyde Hall, Rettendon, nr Chelmsford, Essex
Sissinghurst Castle, Sissinghurst, nr Cranbrook, Kent
Wisley Garden (Royal Horticultural Society), Wisley, Surrey

United States of America
Berry Garden, 11505 Southwest Summerville Avenue, Portland, Oregon
Chehalis Rare Plant Nursery, 2568 Jackson Highway, Chehalis, Washington
Claire Muller, 2001 Ridley, Creele Road, Media, Pennsylvania
Winterthur Gardens, Route 52, Winterthur, Delaware

NURSERIES

Canada

Alpenflora Gardens, 17985 40th Avenue, Surrey (Cloverdale), British Columbia V3S 4N8

Alpenglow Gardens, 13328 King George Highway, North Surrey, British Columbia

India

G. Ghose & Co., Townend, Darjeeling, Bengal

Japan

Mori, Kazuo Alpines, Trinity Garden, 5–8 Matsushita, Nishinomiya, Hyogo PC 662

United Kingdom

Brenda Hyatt Auriculas, 1 Toddington Crescent, Bluebell Hill, nr Chatham, Kent ME5 9QT

Cravens Nursery, 1 Foulds Terrace, Bingley, West Yorkshire BD16 4LZ

Donington Plants, Donington House, Main Road, Wrangle, Boston, Lincolnshire

Edrom Nurseries, Coldingham, Eyemouth, Berwickshire TD14 5TZ

Hartside Nursery Garden, Low Gill House, Alston, Cumbria CA9 3BL

Holden Clough Nursery, Holden, Bolton-by-Bowland, Clitheroe, Lancashire BB7 4PF

Hopleys Plants Ltd, Much Hadham, Hertfordshire SG10 0BU

W. E. Th. Ingwersen Ltd, Birch Farm Nursery, Gravetye, East Grinstead, West Sussex RH19 4LE

The Japanese Garden Co., No. 2 Home Farm, Caton, Lancaster, Lancashire LA2 9NB

Martin Nest Nurseries, Grange Cottage, Harpswell Lane, Hemswell, Gainsborough, Lincolnshire DN21 5UP

Old Inn Cottage Nursery, Old Inn Cottage, Piddington, Bicester, Oxfordshire OX6 OPY

Ramparts Nurseries, Hempster Farm, Berrydown, Combe Martin, Devon

F. R. Shipston, 11 Harvey Close, Allesley, Coventry, West Midlands CV5 9FU

Waincliffe Garden Nursery, 24 Bradford Road, Northowram, Halifax, West Yorkshire

United States of America

Baileys', PO Box 654, Edmonds, Washington 98020

Bartoos Gardens, 6214 South 287th, Kent, Washington 98032

Chehalis Rare Plant Nursery, 2568 Jackson Highway, Chehalis, Washington 98532

Cricklewood Nursery, 11907 Nevers Road, Snohomish, Washington 98290

Darlene Heller, 1685 Highway 995 #42, Mount Vernon, Washington 98273

Grand Ridge Nursery, 27801 Southeast High Point Way, Issaquah, Washington 98027

Lamb Nurseries, East 101 Sharp, Spokane, Washington 99202

Montrose Nursery, PO Box 957, Hillsborough, North Carolina 27278

Mount Tahoma Nursery, 28111 112th Avenue East, Graham, Washington 98338

Nature's Garden, Route 1, Box 488, Beaverton, Oregon 97007

Oliver Nurseries Inc., 1159 Bronson Road, Fairfield, Connecticut 06430

The Plant Farm, 11811 Northeast 73rd, Kirkland, Washington 98033

Primrose Acres, 14015 84th Avenue East, Bothell, Washington 98011

Primrose Lane Nursery, 13631 196th Southeast, Renton, Washington 98056

The Rock Garden, RFD #2, Litchfield, Maine 04350

Russell Graham, 4030 Eagle Crest Road Northwest, Salem, Oregon 97304

Siskiyou Rare Plant Nursery, 2825 Cummings Road, Medford, Oregon 97501

Spring Hill Farm, PO Box 42, Gig Harbor, Washington 98335

Stonecrop Nurseries, Cold Springs, New York, New York 10516

Glossary

anther the pollen-bearing tip of the stamen (*qv*)
body colour the base or foundation colour of the petal in edged varieties
carrot the main root
calyx the external part of the flower, consisting of the sepals; the calyx may be covered in farina (*qv*) or remain green
corolla the petals collectively; usually six to eight petals form the corolla of each flower
farina the powdery coating seen on some auricula flowers, leaves, and stems
footstalk = pedicel (*qv*)
ground colour = body colour (*qv*)
meal = farina (*qv*)
paste the distinctive white ring on the flower of a show auricula
pedicel the small stem that supports an individual pip of the flower truss (*qv*)
pin = stigma (*qv*)
pin-eyed term used of a flower in which the stigma (*qv*) is held above the stamen (*qv*)
pip the floret or individual flower in a truss (*qv*)
scape a florist's term for the stem that supports the flower truss (*qv*)
stamen the male part of the flower – a thin stalk within the tube (*qv*) that carries the anther (*qv*)
stigma the female part of the flower – the tip of the pistil, which receives the pollen
thrum = anther (*qv*)
thrum-eyed term used of a flower in which the stamen (*qv*) and anther (*qv*) are held above the stigma (*qv*) at the mouth of the tube
truss the complete group of pips (*qv*) or florets radiating from the head of the scape (*qv*)
tube the centre of the flower
umbel = truss (*qv*)

Bibliography

Biffen, Rowland H., *The Auricula: the Story of a Florist's Flower*, The Garden Book Club, London, no date [1951]
Clapham, Sidney, *Primulas*, David & Charles, Newton Abbot, 1971
Corsar, Kenneth Charles, *Primulas in the Garden*, The Garden Book Club, London, revised edition 1952
Genders, Roy, *Auriculas*, The Garden Book Club, London, 1958
Haysom, C. G., *Florists' Auriculas and Gold-laced Polyanthus*, W. H. & L. Collingridge Ltd, London, 1957
Hecker, W. R., *Auriculas and Primroses*, B.T. Batsford Ltd, London, 1971
Moreton, C. Oscar, *The Auricula, its History and Character* (*with seventeen coloured plates reproduced from paintings by Rory McEwen*), The Ariel Press, London, 1964
Puttock, A. G., *Primulas*, The Garden Book Club, London, 1957
Smith, G. F., Burrow, B., and Lowe, D. B., *Primulas of Europe and America*, Alpine Garden Society, Woking, 1984
Wemyss-Cooke, Jack, *Primulas Old and New*, David & Charles, Newton Abbot, no date [1986]

Acknowledgements

My first thanks must go to Mr Gordon Douglas, whose encouragement initially instilled in me the determination to make auriculas available to everyone who wished to grow them and whose expert knowledge has been so generously made available to me.

I much appreciate the guidance so willingly given me by Mr J. M. Barlow, a life member of the National Auricula and Primula Society, and the encouragement I have received from Mrs Gwen Baker, Mrs Ruth Duthie, Mr Ed Picken, and Mr Bernard Smith.

Finally, I must thank my eldest daughter, Julie, for undertaking the laborious task of typing my manuscript.

Picture Credits

Mrs H. Blackburn pp. 36, 51(top), 57(top right), 66(top); Mr D. Hadfield p. 44(bottom); Mr A. Hawkes pp. 49(top), 50(bottom), 52, 60(bottom), 73(top); Midland and West Section, National Auricula and Primrose Society pp. 34(bottom), 37(top), 39, 40(top), 49(bottom), 63, 65(top), 71, 72(top); Mr Geoffrey Nicolle p. 78(top), 78(bottom); Dr M. Sheader p. 43(bottom); the Harry Smith Collection pp. 33, 34(top), 41, 48(top), 48(bottom), 50(top), 51(bottom), 54(top), 54(bottom), 55(bottom), 56, 57(centre right), 58(left), 59(left), 59(right), 62(bottom), 67(top), 70(bottom), 74, 75(top), 76(bottom), 79, 80; Mr W. Stewart pp. 35(bottom), 43(top), 44(top), 45(left), 45(right), 53(top), 53(bottom), 55(top), 57(top left), 57(bottom right), 60(top), 61(top), 61(bottom), 64(top), 64(bottom), 65(bottom), 68, 69(bottom), 70(top), 72(bottom), 73(bottom), 75(bottom), 77; Mr P. Talboys pp. 35(top), 37(bottom), 38(top), 38(bottom), 40(bottom), 42(top), 46, 47, 58(right), 62(top), 69(top), 76(top); Mr Derek Telford pp. 42 (bottom), 66(bottom), 67(bottom).

INDEX

Page numbers in *italics* refer to captions to the colour plates.